Tibetan Home Cooking

Tibetan Home Cooking

By

Lobsang Wangdu and Yolanda O'Bannon

Copyright © 2011 by Lobsang Wangdu and Yolanda O'Bannon

First paperback edition, 2018

Direct questions and requests regarding permission to reprint to Lobsang Wangdu or Yolanda O'Bannon at yowangdu@yowangdu.com. Thank you!

All photographs and recipes in this book © Yolanda O'Bannon and Lobsang Wangdu. (All recipes created by Lobsang Wangdu unless otherwise noted in the text.)

All rights reserved. No part of this book may be reproduced in any form by any electronic or mechanical means including photocopying, recording, or information storage and retrieval without permission in writing from the authors, except by a review, who may quote brief passages in review.

We welcome you to visit us at YoWangdu Experience Tibet:

www.yowangdu.com

Contents

Introduction
Some Basic Things to Know about Tibetan Food — 1
Can I Cook Tibetan Food Without Exotic ingredients? — 3

Breads
- *Tingmo*: Steamed buns — 6
- *Amdo balep*: Yeasted round loaf — 10
- *Logo momo*: Fried/steamed bread — 14
- *Numtrak balep*: Deep-fried bread — 17
- *Balep korkun*: Pan bread — 21

For Meat Lovers
- Making Dishes with Mutton — 26
- *Sha momo*: Steamed beef dumplings — 27
- *Labsha*: Radish and beef — 34
- *Sha balep*: Fried beef pies — 38
- *Thukpa gyathuk*: "Chinese" style noodles — 43
- *Shaptra*: Fried beef — 47
- *Sha mothuk*: Beef dumplings in soup — 50
- *Rutang*: Beef-based soup — 58
- *Shaptse*: Beef with cabbage — 60
- *Shamdrey*: Beef + rice + potatoes — 64
- *Drothuk*: Beef porridge — 70

Contents

For Veggie Lovers
Shamey momo: Steamed vegetable dumplings	74
Shamey balep: Fried pies with vegetable filling	81
Shameytse: Cabbage and shiitake mushrooms	87
Shamey mothuk: Vegetable dumplings in soup	91
Trang tsel: Fresh salad	97

A Little Something for Everyone
Thentuk: "Pull" noodle soup	101
Pa: *Tsampa* with butter tea	106
Sepen: Hot sauce	110
Po cha: Tibetan (Butter) tea	114
Thukpa bhathuk: Soup with small hand-made pasta	117

Sweets
Dresil: Sweet rice	124
Bhatsa marku: Buttered small hand-made pasta	126

Acknowledgments	130
About the Authors	131

Introduction

Tibetan food, which evolved to sustain a hardy people living at an average elevation of 16,000 feet, is like no other food in the world. Who else but Tibetans have a great time drinking salty tea and eating sweet rice in the same sitting? Or grow up on a steady diet of roasted barley flour made into a dough with tea, butter, sugar and dried cheese from the female yak (*dri*)? While these dishes can be an acquired taste for non-Tibetans, there is a wealth of other uniquely Tibetan flavors that inspire total devotion in food lovers around the world. Tibetan dumplings — momos — have their own massively popular page on Facebook, which has a mission "to spread the knowledge about momos, possibly the best dish in the world."

We have written *Tibetan Home Cooking* to share with you the most common, well-loved Tibetan foods that are cooked in Tibetan homes, both inside Tibet and around the world. Each recipe in this book is authentically Tibetan, created by Lobsang Wangdu and a small group of excellent Tibetan chefs, featuring Tsering Tamding la. Each recipe is based on the cook's personal history with a particular well-known Tibetan dish, usually passed down in the family for hundreds of years. We hope you will find as much joy in these recipes as we have, and welcome all your feedback at yowangdu@yowangdu.com.

Wishing you the joys of Tibetan cooking,
Lobsang Wangdu and Yolanda O'Bannon

Barley fields by a village in Central Tibet.

Some Basic Things to Know about Tibetan Food

- The staple food of Tibet is *tsampa*, which is flour made from roasted highland barley. Tibetans in fact, are collectively referred to as *tsampa*-eaters (*po mi tsamsey*). The most common way to eat *tsampa* is in *pa* which is made from *tsampa*, and various combinations of tea, butter, sugar and dried cheese.

- There's no such thing as "yak butter" or "yak cheese." Only the male of the species is called a yak in Tibet. The females, called *dri*, produce the butter, cheese, yogurt and milk used in Tibetan cooking, so what is commonly referred to as "yak" cheese or butter is actually *dri* butter or *dri* cheese.

- Tibetans are not typically vegetarian, and are in fact heavy meat eaters, eating primarily yak, beef, mutton, and goat. While the great majority of Tibetans are Tibetan Buddhists, they are not vegetarian. Most likely due to the difficulty of raising a wide variety of vegetables on the Tibetan plateau, Tibetan diets (at least in Central Tibet) have traditionally focused on *tsampa* dishes and meat, when the household could afford it.

- Tibetans do not traditionally eat fish. Although there are amazing rivers and lakes full of fish in many areas of Tibet, the people don't typically eat fish or sea food. A commonly held belief is that it is better to eat large animals than fish or small animals, since less lives need to be sacrificed to feed the same amount of people.

- Generally speaking, Tibetan food reflects what can survive at Tibet's average elevation of 16,000 feet (4900 meters). Highland barley is the most important grain, followed by varieties of wheat, while only the hardier vegetables tend to thrive in Tibet, like cabbage, radish, turnip, green peas, carrot, potato, mustard and green onion. In the countryside, radish and potatoes would be preserved year round by keeping them in a deepish hole dug in the family house compound, covered by hay.

Can I Cook Tibetan Food Without Exotic Ingredients?

Absolutely! While Tibetan food has a reputation for being quite exotic, the great majority of the recipes in *Tibetan Home Cooking* can be made completely with common ingredients and kitchen utensils. There are some unusual ingredients, but almost none of them are essential to make the Tibetan Home Cooking recipes. Below are some of the ingredients that you may be challenged to find, and some ideas on where to buy them, or how to substitute for them.

Tsampa

Our *pa* recipe does require *tsampa*, roasted barley flour, which most of you won't find in your corner market :-) There are a few shops we can recommend. Please let them know we sent you :-)
- One is our friend Dhondup la, who sells *tsampa* online at: http://www.tibetantsampa.com/
- We can also recommend buying from Ann at Purple Mountain Tsampa, who makes *tsampa* fresh to order from hull-less barley, a "whole food" barley grown without a hull, and nutritionally superior to "pearled" or "hulled barley." Contact Ann at annlachman@gmail.com.
- If you are in the San Francisco Bay Area, our friend Samten la sells bags of *tsampa* from her Cafe Tibet restaurant in Berkeley, California. (2020 University, Berkeley, CA (510) 548-5553)

Dri Cheese and Butter (Commonly called "Yak" Cheese and Butter)

The butter and dried cheese which we refer to in the recipes for *pa* and *bhatsa marku* comes from the milk of the female yak, the *dri*. We have not found any sources outside of Tibet that sell these. Tibetans in exile get them directly from relatives inside Tibet. However, we can substitute some hard western cheese for the dried *dri* cheese. Parmesan, Asiago, or Romano cheeses work fairly well, though they do not actually taste like *dri* cheese, which is quite unique. Still, the texture is close enough, and they work well as substitutes.

Yak Meat

Tsampa

Chu ship—Dried dri cheese in small pieces

Yak meat is the most commonly eaten meat in Tibet, and is prepared any number of ways, including raw and dried, as well as in the popular momo dishes, noodle soups and labsha. The only way we know that we and others in the Tibetan community get yak meat is to go to Tibet or to get some dried yak from travelling Tibetans. As a substitute everyone uses beef, as we do here for our meat recipes. We have seen some yak meat for sale online but have not tried this ourselves. The meat is quite mild and lean.

Yerma, or *Emma* (Commonly called Szechuan pepper)

Tibetans often use this very tasty, tiny, slightly numbing and citrusy "pepper" in hot sauces, meat dishes and in *trang tsel*. It is commonly called Szechuan pepper, but is actually a fruit. You should experiment with very small quantities and grind the dried peppercorns very well with a mortar and pestle before using. *Emma* is sort of like Japanese wasabi in that you don't want to get a big piece of it in one bite. The amounts we use in the recipes does not leave your mouth numb unless you happen to get a whole pod, which you can avoid by grinding the *emma* well and mixing the ground mixture well with the other ingredients.Look for dried "Szechuan" or "Sichuan" pepper or "prickly ash" in Asian food stores. We have not tried this shop so cannot give a recommendation, but we found *emma* for sale online here: http://www.savoryspiceshop.com/spices/pprcrnszech.html

Droma Root

Droma is a small, highly nutritious root that is harvested on the grasslands of Tibet and eaten especially for Tibetan holidays, like *Losar* (Tibetan New Year), as we mention in our *dresil* (sweet rice) recipe. Unfortunately, it is another ingredient that we have not found except in Tibet or perhaps the markets of Nepal. Although *droma* is tasty and unusual (sort of similar to a tiny sweet potato), don't worry if you can't get it, since most Tibetans outside Tibet also don't have good access to it, and tend to eat their *dresil* without it.

Yak Meat

Emma

Droma

Bok Choy

We use bok choy or baby bok choy in our *momo* recipes, as well as for *sha* and *shamey balep*. Bok choy, also called Chinese chard or Chinese cabbage, is a crisp green with edible stems and leaves that is available in most Asian markets. As a substitute, you can use Napa cabbage, broccoli, Swiss chard, celery or collard greens. (We don't recommend mustard greens.) Of course each of these will taste a bit different than bok choy, but what we're aiming for when we add them to momos or *balep* is a blended flavor with the meat or other vegetables, so it's not a problem.

Labu — Daikon

The large white radish that much of the world knows as daikon and that Tibetans call *labu* apparently originated in continental Asia. Tibetans use it in noodle soups, and cooked with yak, beef and mutton. Like bok choy, you can find daikon in almost any Asian food store. If you are not near one, there are substitutes. For our *thenthuk* and *thukpa bhathuk* recipes, you could use red radish or turnips. We have also used potatoes at times, though you have to be sure they don't cook down too much. For the *labsha* recipe, we suggest trying red radish, though the typical red radish will be spicier than the mild daikon, or jicama, if you can get that.

Dumpling Wrappers

We offer instructions on how to hand-make all the wrappers for all the recipes in this book, but if you don't have time to make the dumpling wrappers yourself, you can buy round dumpling wrappers in many major grocery stores. They might also be called wonton, potsticker, gyoza or shu mai wrappers. These will taste a bit different than the kind we make, but they will work. If needed, you can also buy square wrappers and cut the corners to make them round, or just experiment with square shapes.

Shiitake Mushrooms

Shiitake mushrooms have a wonderful earthy flavor and we use them as a substitute for Tibetan mushrooms, *sesha*, which we cannot get outside of Tibet. For our recipes you can use fresh or dried shiitake mushrooms. Just soak the dried ones for 30 minutes before using. If you cannot find shiitakes, you can use crimini mushrooms, straw mushrooms, chanterelles, or just good old white mushrooms instead.

Bok Choy   *Labu Daikon*   Dumpling Wrappers   Shiitake Mushrooms

Breads

tingmo

Steamed Buns

by Tsering Tamding la

Relatively quick and easy to make, *tingmo* are very commonly cooked in Tibetan homes. Inside Tibet, they are often eaten at breakfast with rice porridge (*dreythuk*), while in exile, *tingmo* are more likely to be eaten with hot sauce along with lunch or dinner. Tsering Tamding la, creator of this recipe, likes to make smaller than average tingmos. "If you look at the big ones," he jokes, "you're already full"!

tingmo

For 4 people

You will need:
- Rolling board and pin
- Steamer

Ingredients
- 1/8 teaspoon active dry yeast
- 1 cup warm water (100° to 110° Fahrenheit)
- 2 and 1/2 cups of all-purpose flour
- 1/4 teaspoon baking powder
- 1/4 teaspoon salt, or to your taste

Prepare the Dough
- Mix well the flour, baking powder and salt.
- In a separate small bowl, add yeast to 1 cup of warm water (100° to 110° Fahrenheit).
- Let stand for 10 minutes, until yeast is foamy.
- Or, just follow the directions on your yeast package :-)
- When the yeast is foamy, add the yeast mixture slowly to the flour mixture, mixing gently with your hand, until you have a smooth ball of dough.
- Let the dough rest for 1/2 hour.

tingmo

Making the *Tingmo* Shapes

- Put a little flour on a rolling board.
- Roll it out to a big circle about 1/3 inch thick. It should be thicker than you would make it for momos.
- Cut the circle of dough in half, right along the line of the circumference, then into long strips.
- Roll the long strips into little buns in various shapes. See photos and the video for two basic shapes, but you can use your imagination to make whatever shapes you think are nice.

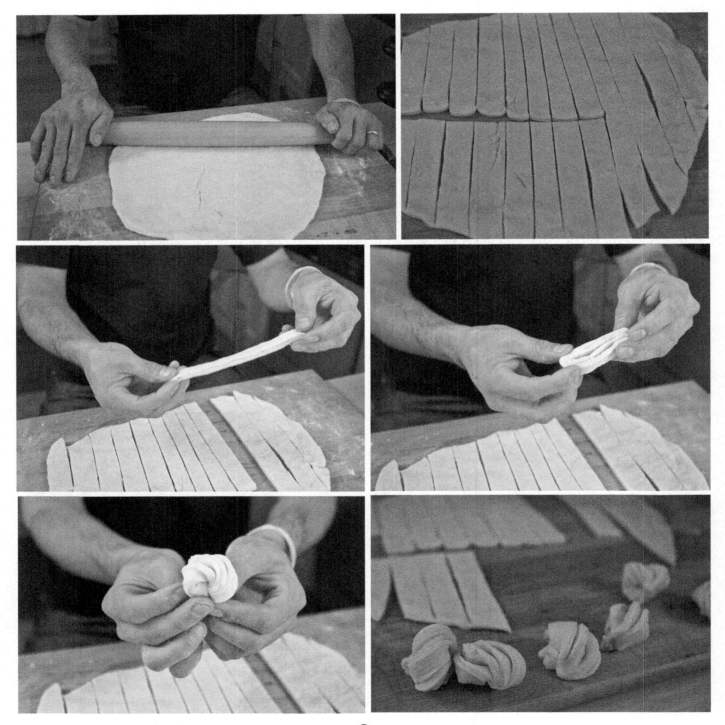

tingmo

Steam the Tingmos

- Bring water to a boil in the steamer.
- Lightly oil the steaming layer(s) of your steamer. (We use spray oil.)
- We are using a double steamer, but any steamer is fine.
- Place the *tingmo* in the steamer, not touching each other.
- Once the water is boiling, place the racks with the *tingmo* in your steamer, and steam for 12 minutes.

Serve hot. You can reheat in microwave or in a pan on the stovetop, but these are best fresh out of the steamer!

amdo balep

Amdo Bread

These crusty round yeasted loaves take their name from the Amdo region of northeastern Tibet, but are popular also in central Tibet. In both regions, the bakers will sometimes cover the dough in the ashes of a fire instead of using an oven or stove. Though we use yeast here, Tibetans will also make this bread with baking powder or a kind of starter. We also mix whole wheat and white flour, though some would use only white flour. Traditionally, in Tibet, the loaves were most likely a kind of whole wheat, as refined wheats did not exist in many places due to a lack of the necessary milling equipment. Our friend Lungtok la told us that in his home town in Amdo, the village people would make huge *balep* on special occasions—so large that two people could hardly lift them!

amdo balep

One round loaf for 4 people

Note: Prepare the dough the night before you want to cook it, or at least 3 hours before cooking.

Ingredients
- 1 cup of warm water (between 100° to 110° fahrenheit) (Note that in the video Lobsang initially puts about 2/3 cup of warm water with the yeast, and after the yeast foams, he adds another 1/3 cup to make a cup total. You can just start with 1 cup of warm water.)
- Additional 1/2 cup water (Out of the tap is fine.)
- 1 teaspoon active dry yeast
- 1/2 teaspoon sugar to activate the yeast
- 1.5 cups whole wheat flour
- 1.5 cups all purpose white flour
- 1 tablespoon cooking oil (We use Canola.)

Traditional water mill, still in use, near Shigatse to make flour for wheat, barley and green peas.

amdo balep

Prepare the Yeast

- Add the yeast and sugar to 1 cup of warm water.
- Let stand for 10 minutes until yeast is quite foamy.
- Or, follow the directions on your yeast package.
- Sometimes, the yeast does not activate and you have to try with some new yeast.

Prepare the Dough

- Combine the whole wheat and white flour and mix well together.
- Pour yeast mixture (which should be about 1 cup) and an additional 1/2 cup of water (tap water is fine) into a bowl with the combined whole wheat and white flour.
- Mix well and knead for about 5 minutes to form a smooth ball of dough.
- With your hands, press the dough out into a flat circle. If your pan is 10 inches like ours, your circle would be 8-9 inches. If your pan is smaller, then make your circle an inch or two smaller than your pan. The thickness doesn't matter because the dough will rise.
- Spread 1 tablespoon cooking oil around the bottom of a pan, and place the dough in the pan. (we use a 10 inch non-stick pan. You can use a smaller pan or any pan, but the sides should be straight vertically for ease of turning the bread and removing it from the pan.)
- Put a lid on the pan and let rise in a warmish place for a minimum of two hours. We prepare it the night before and let it sit overnight. The dough should approximately double in size.

amdo balep

Cooking

- Once the dough is doubled, or at least 2 hours later, put the pan on the stove on high heat and cook the *balep*, covered, for 3 minutes, then turn down to medium-low (4 out of 10 on our stove) and cook for 6 more minutes. Of course your stove may be different so monitor the *balep* to be sure it's not burning :-)
- After that, turn the heat down to the lowest heat, for another 2 minutes.
  This makes a total of 11 minutes for the first side.
- Being careful not to burn yourself, turn the bread over using a plate, then turn the heat back up to medium low (3 out of 10 on the settings on our stove), and cook for 8 minutes.
- Turn heat down to low (1 out of 10) for another 6 minutes. Total cooking time for the second side is 14 minutes.
- Total cooking time is 25 minutes: first side 11 minutes and second side 14 minutes, on our stove. Yours may be a little more or less.
- Take it off the stove and serve. If not serving right away cool on a rack.
- Best to eat hot!

logo momo

Pan Fried and Steamed Bread

Logo Momo is a very typical Tibetan bread, which is both fried and steamed, which seems to be unique to Tibet, as we've never seen this in any other culture's bread. Though unusual, it is simple and easy to make. In Tibet, l*ogo momo* would be eaten at lunch or dinner, with some vegetables or maybe *shaptra* (fried meat). In central Tibet, people eat *logo momo* with a big piece of cooked yak meat that each person gets a chunk of and cuts pieces from, dipping the meat in *sepen*.

logo momo   ཨོ་སྒོར་མོག་མོག་

For 2 people

Ingredients

- 2 cups white all-purpose flour
- 1/2 teaspoon dry active yeast
- Pinch of sugar
- 1/2 cups water (total)
- 1 tablespoon cooking oil (We use Canola.)

Prepare the Yeast

- Add yeast and sugar to 1/4 cup of warm water (100° to 110° Fahrenheit)
- Let stand for 10 minutes, until yeast is foamy
- Or, just follow the directions on your yeast package.

Prepare the Dough

- Combine the yeast mixture with the flour and another 1/4 cup of water
- Mix very well by hand and knead to form a smooth ball of dough. The dough should be quite stiff, as it will need to hold the logo momo shape.
- Cover with a lid, or with plastic, and let rest for 2-3 hours.

logo momo

Shape the *Logo Momo*

- After resting, the dough should be flexible but stiff enough to hold an igloo shape, or an upside-down bowl
- Divide the dough in half.
- Roll each half into a ball.
- With your fingers, press out the center of the ball to make a bowl shape. (See the video for this.) The walls should not be too thick, maybe 3/4 to 1 inch thick. If too thick, it's difficult to cook the dough through.

Cooking

- Heat 1 tablespoon of cooking oil in a non-stick pan to high.
- When oil is heated, add the logo momos, with the hole facing down, to the pan.

numtrak balep

Deep-Fried Bread

By Tsering Tamding la

This puffy deep-fried bread is wildly delicious when served piping hot. It is special occasion food, especially in Tibet, where for many the large amounts of oil would be considered expensive. In exile, *numtrak balep* might be offered to guests on the morning of ceremonial days. For breakfast, you might have it with some tea, or at lunch, paired with some vegetables.

numtrak balep

For 5 people

Ingredients

- 5 cups white all-purpose flour (referred to as "AP" flour in the video)
- 1/2 tablespoon sugar
- 1/2 tablespoon salt, or to your taste
- 1/2 tablespoon baking powder
- About 1 and 1/2 cups water. You may need a bit more.
- Enough cooking oil for deep frying

numtrak balep

You will need:
- Pan appropriate for deep frying
- Large slotted or netted utensil that you can lift and drain the deep-fried *balep* with.

Preparing the Dough
- Mix flour, sugar, salt and baking powder well together.
- With your hand, mix in the water slowly, in little amounts. Add more if your dough is dry-ish.
- Knead to a smooth ball of dough.
- Cover in plastic and let sit for 30 minutes.

Shaping the Dough
- Roll out the dough on a flat surface to make a thick rope.
- Break off fistfuls of dough to make about 10 pieces of dough.
- Roll out each piece with a rolling pin, to a circle about ¼ inch high and 6-7 inches in diameter.
- (You can make bigger or smaller circles if you wish.)
- Cut 2 or 3 parallel slits in the middle of the dough.

numtrak balep

Cooking

- Put 2 and 1/2 inches of oil in a deepish pan for deep frying.
- Heat the oil to high.
- When it is hot, ease each *balep* slowly into the oil.
- When you can see that the edges of the bottom are a golden brown (you can see the edges of the bottom when you are looking at the *balep* in the oil), turn the *balep* over. This should take less than a minute.
- The *balep* will rise to the top of the oil. You can push it back down with a utensil for a moment. It will be done in probably 30-40 seconds.
- Pick it up with a large slotted or netted utensil and let the oil drain back into the pan. Gently raise the *balep* up and down to allow more excess oil to drain off.
- Drain well and put on a large dish covered with paper towels to soak some of the oil. (There will still be plenty left ;-)

balep korkun

Pan Bread

Tibetans make so many kinds of bread, but these small, round breads are among the very easiest to make. This recipe is very popular in Central Tibet, where it is made at home, but also easily purchased at little shops or stalls on the street. Lobsang's recipe combines whole wheat and white flour, because we like the taste of the whole wheat, and the way that the white flour keeps the bread softer and higher rising. In Tibet, these days, *balep korkun* is almost exclusively white bread, though traditionally, in the days before more modern milling machinery, they would have been whole wheat. In Lhasa, *balep korkun* is sold either sweet or plain. The sweet versions, which carry a small red mark, are made with *purang*, which we believe is concentrated sugar cane juice, like Indian *jaggery*.

balep korkun

For 2 people.

Ingredients
- 1 cup whole wheat flour
- 1 cup all-purpose white flour
- 1 tablespoon baking powder
- 1 cup water

Two young girls selling *balep korkun* in Lhasa.

balep korkun

Preparing the Dough

It is better to start preparing the dough the night before or at least 2 hours before cooking, to rest the dough, but in a pinch 15-20 minutes is okay.)

- For the most simple version of this bread, you mix the two flours and the baking powder together well.
- Add a little water, while mixing by hand, and keep adding water, about one cup total, until you can make a smooth ball of dough.
- Knead the dough very well until the dough is flexible, 3-5 minutes.
- After you finish kneading, leave the dough in a container with a lid on it or place it in a plastic bag, and let sit, ideally for at least two hours, or overnight. If you don't have that amount of time, then let the dough rest for 15-20 minutes before rolling it out.
- After the dough has rested, separate it into about 6 pieces and roll them into ball shapes.
- Place one of the ball shapes on a flat surface and roll it out with a rolling pin, making a flat, round shape about 1/4 inch to 1/3 inch high (you can test thicker ones if you like). Repeat with all your dough.

balep korkun

Cooking

- Normally, we cook the *balep* in a large non-stick pan with no oil.
- First you should heat up your frying pan until it gets hot.
- Add the *balep* and cook them on the first side on high for about 2 minutes, then turn down the heat to medium and cook another 3 minutes.
- Rotate the *balep* a few times so they heat more evenly.
- Now turn over the bread, and cook another five minutes on medium heat, so both sides get cooked well.

Serve hot!

Notes:

- We mix the two flours because we like the health factor of whole wheat but if you only use wheat, it doesn't rise very well.
- If you like, you can add a bit of butter, or applesauce to the flour before you begin adding the water, for special flavor and to make it a bit softer. Tibetans don't commonly do this, but it is nice for a change from time to time.

Making Dishes with Mutton

While we prefer beef and have made all of the meat recipes with various cuts of beef, Tibetans also commonly eat mutton. All of the following recipes are very frequently prepared with mutton, and if you wish, simply substitute mutton where the recipe calls for beef.

- *labsha*
- *shaptra*
- *rutang*
- *shaptse*
- *shamdrey*
- *drothuk*
- *thukpa bathuk*
- *thenthuk*

This sheep is no mutton — he has a happy life as a pet in Lhasa :-)

sha momo

Beef Dumplings (Steamed)

Utterly unique and delicious, Tibetan dumplings are basically the unofficial national dish of Tibet. Every Tibetan family has a slightly different *momo* recipe, with various theories on how to make them the most juicy and delicious, or how to keep the dough skins to the desired delicate thinness. The variations are endless – momos can be meat, veg, steamed (the most popular), fried, and cooked in soup. Typically, in Tibet the meat *momo* would be made from yak meat, but outside of Tibet people use ground beef instead. In case you're wondering, the word "*momo*" is pronounced with the same "o" sound as in "so-so."

sha momo

For 2 people (Makes about 25 momos.)

Dough Ingredients
- 2 cups white all-purpose flour
- 3/4 cup water
- If you don't have time to make the dumpling wrappers yourself, you can buy round dumpling wrappers in many major grocery stores. Might also be called wonton, potsticker, gyoza or shu mai wrappers. These will taste differently than the kind we make, but they will work.

Filling Ingredients
- 1/2 pound ground beef (not too lean)
- 1 cup baby bok choy (about 2 clusters) or cabbage
- 1/2 large onion (We used a red onion.)
- 1 and 1/2 tablespoons fresh ginger
- 4 cloves of garlic
- 1/2 cup cilantro
- 2 stalks green onion
- 1/2 teaspoon salt, or to your taste
- 1 tablespoon of soy sauce
- 1/2 tablespoon beef bouillon
- 1 tablespoon of water
- 1/4 cup of cooking oil (We use Canola.)

Optional:
- 1/4 teaspoon ground *emma* (Commonly called Szechuan pepper.)

sha momo

Prepare the Dough
- Mix 2 cups white all-purpose flour and 3/4 cup of water very well by hand and knead until you make a smooth ball of dough.
- Knead the dough very well until the dough is quite flexible.
- Leave your dough in the pot with the lid on, or in a plastic bag, while you prepare the rest of the ingredients. You should not let the dough dry out, or it will be hard to work with.

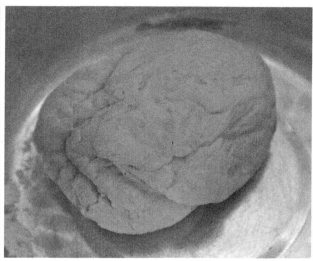

Prepare the Filling
- Chop the bok choy, onion, ginger, garlic, cilantro and green onion into very, very small pieces.
- If you are using *emma*, which is optional, grind it with a mortar and pestle into pieces that are as small as you can get them. *Emma* is sort of like Japanese *wasabi* in that you don't want to get a big piece of it in your momo.
- Mix the beef with all the other filling ingredients by hand together very well in a large bowl. (Including the tablespoon of water)

sha momo

Making the *Momo* Dough Circles

- When your dough and filling are both ready, it is time for the tricky part of making the dumpling shapes. Place the dough on a chopping board and use a rolling pin to roll it out quite thinly, about 1/8 inch thick. It should not be so thin that you can see through it when you pick it up.

- After you have rolled out the dough, you will need to cut it into little circles for each *momo*. The easiest way to do this is turn a small cup or glass upside down to cut out circles about the size of the palm of your hand. (We use a cup 3 and 1/4 inches in diameter.) With this method, you don't have to worry about making good circles of dough because each one will be the same size and shape.

- Of course, you can also make the circles by the more traditional, and more difficult, way of pinching off a small ball of dough and rolling each ball in your palms until you have a smooth ball of dough. Then, you can use a rolling pin to flatten out the dough into a circle, making the edges more thin than the middle. This is much harder to do, and takes more time, though most Tibetans still use this method.

- Now that you have a small, flat, circular piece of dough, you are ready to add the filling and make the *momo* shapes. There are many different choices for *momo* shapes, but for these meat momos we will use a very common round shape. If you want to learn about the pretty half-moon shape, see the *shamey* (veggie) *momo* recipe. Don't worry if your first momos don't look so gorgeous — it takes a fair amount of practice to make the beautiful traditional shapes. If you try the classic ones, and they come out a little misshapen, not to worry, they will still taste fabulous! And there's no rule that says you have to make the traditional shapes – get creative with your shapes if you like :-)

sha momo

Shaping a Round *Momo*

- Hold the momo in one hand and with the other hand, begin to pinch the edge of the dough together. (See photo) You don't need to pinch much dough in the first pinch — just enough to make a small fold between your thumb and forefinger.
- Now you will have a little piece of dough pinched together, and you should continue pinching around the circle little by little, keeping your thumb in place, and continuing along the edge of the circle with your forefinger, grabbing the next little piece of dough, and folding and pinching it down into the original fold/pinch being held by your thumb. Basically you will be pinching the whole edge of the circle into one spot.
- Continue folding and pinching all around the edge of the circle until you come back around to where you started and then close the hole with a final pinch. Make sure you close the hole on top of the *momo*. That way you don't lose the juicy part of the *momo* :-)
- As you are making your momos, you will need to have a non-stick surface and a damp cloth or lid handy to keep the momo's you've made from drying out while you're finishing the others. You can lay the momos in the lightly-greased steamer and keep the lid on them, or you can lay them on wax paper and cover them with the lightly damp cloth.

sha momo

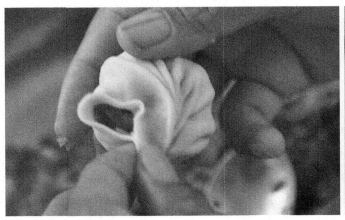
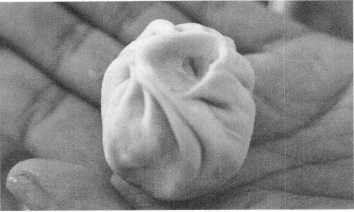

Cook up Your Momos!

- Finally, you should boil water in a large steamer. (Tibetans often use a double or triple decker steamer, to make many momos at one time.)
- Oil the steamer surface lightly before putting the momos in, so they won't stick to the metal. We use spray oil.
- Place the momos a little distance apart in the steamer as they will expand a little bit when they cook. They should not be touching.
- After the water is already boiling, place the stemer layer holding the momos on the pot.
- Steam the momos for about 12 minutes, with the water boiling on high heat.
- The meat filling should be cooked all the way through, with no pinkness.

sha momo

Serving

- Serve the momos right off the stove, with the dipping sauce of your choice. At home, we mix together soy sauce and Patak's Hot Lime Relish, which we get in Indian stores, or the Asian section of supermarkets. Tibetan hot sauce is also very good.
- Be careful when you take the first bite of the hot momos since the juice is very, very hot, and can burn you easily.
- Momos are very good for your social life. When we are making momos, we chat and have a lot of fun. And they taste great!

labsha

Beef and White Radish

By Tsering Tamding la

Labu, the large white Tibetan radish, is apparently a cousin of the Japanese daikon, and though the world knows this tasty root by its Japanese name, it originated in continental Asia (http://en.wikipedia.org/wiki/Daikon). Although *labsha* might sound sort of plain, it was one of the tastiest dishes we made while creating this eBook. It may be that the beef and radish seem to flavor each other. The beef gets coated in the radish and the radish seems to soak up some of the meat juice. Anyway, we don't know why, but *labsha* tastes amazing.

labsha

For 2 people

Ingredients

- 2 medium *labu* (Tibetan word for what is commonly called daikon, or Japanese radish) = 1.1 pounds unpeeled
- 1 pound beef (We used cross rib roast.)
- 1 medium onion (We use red.)
- 1 tomato
- 2 cloves garlic
- 1/4 cup cilantro, chopped
- 1 teaspoon salt, or to your taste
- 1 cup water from the tap, 1/2 cup at a time.
- 1 tablespoon cooking oil (We use Canola or safflower.)

Optional:

- 1/4 teaspoon *emma* (Commonly called Szechuan pepper.)

labsha

Preparation

- Peel the 2 medium *labu* with a knife or potato peeler.
- Discard the hard top ends of the *labuk* and chop the rest into bite-sized pieces. (They will cook down a bit and become smaller.)
- Cut the tomato in half. Slice fairly thin each half, then cut once perpendicular to the slice cuts, to end up with fairly large but thin pieces. (Or however you want :-)
- Mince 2 cloves of garlic
- Chop 1/4 cup cilantro for garnish.
- If using *emma*, roughly grind 1/4 teaspoon of it using a mortar and pestle.
- Chop 1 medium onion
- Chop the beef into bite-sized pieces.

labsha

Cooking

- Heat 1 tablespoon of cooking oil on high.
- Stir fry the garlic and *emma* (optional) for a minute or less, until the edges are a little brown
- Add onions, and stir fry on high for about a minute
- Add beef and stir fry everything added so far on high for about 3 minutes.
- Now add 1/2 cup of cold water (from the tap is fine) and 1 teaspoon of salt, and stir in the *labu* and tomato. Keep the heat on high until the broth starts to boil, then turn down to medium.
- Cover and cook 10-12 minutes on medium.
- Add another 1/2 cup of cold water, then cook again for 9-10 minutes until beef and *labuk* are cooked. Depending on how hard your radish is, you may need to coook longer. Maybe even twice as long or more.
- How do you know it is cooked? The *labu* should be soft. When the *labu* is soft, the beef will be done. In fact the *labu* will be disintegrating a bit, sort of melting, and coating the beef a bit as you stir, creating an amazing flavor on the beef.
- When done cooking, turn off heat and add cilantro for garnish.

Serve with rice or *tingmo* or *numtrak balep*. *Labsha* is sometimes served as an appetizer in Tibet.

sha balep

Fried Meat Pies

Incredibly delicious, *sha balep*, literally "meat bread," are savory, hot, juicy meat pies. Along with momos, these will be the first to go at any Tibetan potluck gathering. Some people in Central Tibet eat them for breakfast, but they are more typically served with lunch or dinner, often with a basic *rutang* soup. You won't be sorry you went to the effort to make these!

sha balep

For 6 people

Dough Ingredients
- 8 cups all-purpose flour (no self-rising flour, baking powder or yeast)
- 3 cups of cold water (Don't use warm or hot water. Water out of the tap is fine.)

Filling Ingredients
- 2 pounds ground beef (We use lower fat beef, but not the extremely low fat one, since we want some juiciness!)
- 2 cups chopped baby bok choy. You can also use cabbage.
- 1/3 cup minced ginger
- 1/4 cup minced garlic
- 1 cup chopped cilantro
- 2 stalks green onion (1/2 cup chopped)
- 1 and 1/4 cup chopped onion (We use red onion.)
- 2 tablespoons of soy sauce
- 1 teaspoon of salt, or to your taste
- 1 tablespoon of beef bouillon
- 2 tablespoons of cooking oil (We use Canola.)

Optional
- 1/2 tablespoon of *emma* (Also called Szechuan pepper.)

sha balep

Dough Preparation
Start two hours before cooking
- Mix flour and water, forming a ball
- Knead at least 5 minutes until dough is smooth and flexible
- Place dough in a dish with a lid, or cover with plastic, or put in a plastic bag.
- Let rest for 2 or more hours so that the dough will be softer when shaping the *balep*.
- Ultimately you want the dough to be soft enough to roll out and to stick together when you pinch together the edges of the *balep*, and hard enough to form a smooth ball and not to stick to the rolling surface. Don't worry too much if your dough is too hard or too soft. If too soft you can add some more flour and/or put more flour on your rolling surface. If it's too hard, you can add more water and re-knead. You don't have to let it sit another two hours in that case.

Roll out Dough
- Roll out the dough on a lightly floured surface with a rolling pin to about 1/8 inch thickness.
- Use an inverted glass or cut out circles (diameter of the circles is approximately 3.5 inches, or 8 centimeters.) Set the circles of dough aside.
- As you cut out the circles you will be left with the dough outside the circles. Pick it back up, form it into a ball and repeat rolling it out until you have nothing left.
- Note: Many Tibetans make the circles one by one by making a small ball of dough and then rolling out each one, but we're lazy and we're not good at rolling them out one by one, so we use the cup.

sha balep

Fill and Shape the *Balep*

- Place a heaping tablespoon or so of filling on one circle of dough, then place a second circle of dough on top of the first one.
- Pinch the edges together very firmly — going all around the circle.
- Then, start anywhere on the circle, fold over a small piece of the edge, and pinch it down, repeating this all around the circle.
- Keep the *balep* you have finished on a lightly oiled flat dish or surface, to avoid the dough sticking on to the surface. If the *balep* are going to be sitting for a long time, you can place a damp cloth over them to keep them from drying out.

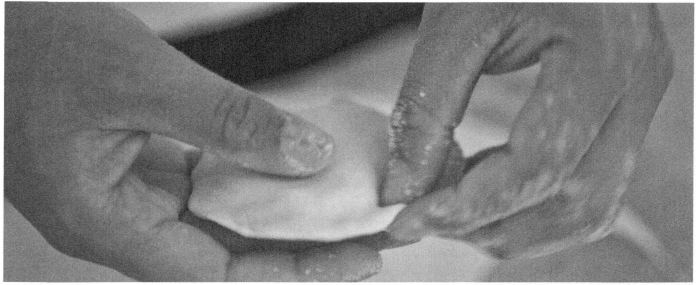

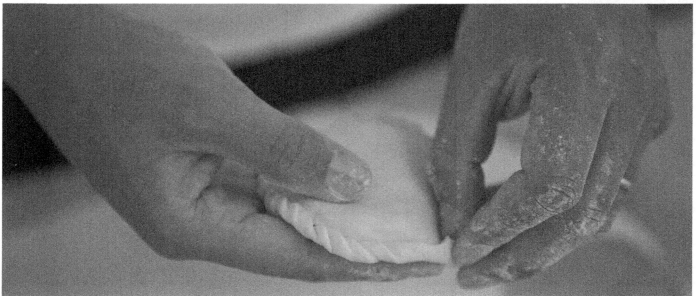

sha balep

Cook
- Heat 2 tablespoons of oil in a large pan until the oil is very hot and then place one layer of balep in the pan and and lower heat to medium. You don't want to burn the outsides before the inside is cooked.
- Cook until golden brown on both sides, turning frequently. Cook about 6-7 minutes for each side, for a total of 12-14 minutes. The meat must cook through.
- Be prepared to turn the fan on or to open the windows as the cooking process can be quite greasy and hot.

Serve
- *Balep* go well with something light, like our *trang tsel* salad.
- For a dipping sauce, try Patak's lime pickle mixed with some soy sauce, or Tibetan hot sauce.

thukpa gyathuk

Chinese-style Noodles

In the winter in Lhasa, Lobsang's aunt and uncle used to bring egg and flour to a place with noodle-making machines that would create the thin, round spaghetti-like noodles used for the *thukpa gyathuk*. *Thukpa* refers to noodles in general, and also to noodle soups or starchy porridges, like rice or barley porridges, and *gyathuk* means "Chinese noodles," so this noodle soup is Chinese style.

thukpa gyathuk

For 2 people

Broth Ingredients

- 1 and 1/4 pounds beef chuck ribs or oxtail
- 1/4 teaspoon *emma* (Commonly called Szechuan pepper.)
- 1 tablespoon soy sauce
- 1/2 cube bouillon = ~ 1 teaspoon
- 2 stalks green onion or 1/4 cup of cilantro (or both)
- 5 cups water

Other Ingredients

- 1/2 pound ground beef
- 9 ounces green beans
- 2 cloves garlic
- 1 tablespoon ginger
- 1/2 medium onion
- 1 medium tomato
- 1/2 tablespoon soy sauce
- 1/4 teaspoon salt, or to your taste
- 6 ounces (uncooked) packaged noodles (Spaghetti noodles are perfect, not wide noodles)
- 1 teaspoon of cooking oil to separate the noodles
- 1 tablespoon cooking oil

thukpa gyathuk

Prepare the Broth
- Place all the broth ingredients except the onion and cilantro in a deepish pot, on high heat. You don't need any cooking oil.
- Bring to a boil.
- When the broth starts to boil, turn down the heat to low, and simmer for 2-3 hours. Or, if you don't have that much time, let simmer for 30 to 40 minutes at least. Tibetans say that it should simmer all day, and the longer the better.

Prepare the Rest of the Ingredients
- When your broth is close to ready, chop the onion and tomato.
- Mince the ginger and garlic.
- Cut the green beans into diagonal sections about 2 inches long.
- Cut the green onions for garnish and set aside in a separate dish.

Cook the Noodles
- We use spaghetti, but you can use any thin long noodle. (Don't use a wide noodle.)
- Follow directions on your noodle package to prepare your noodles.

thukpa gyathuk

Cook the Beef and Beans
- Heat cooking oil in a pan to high.
- Stir fry garlic, ginger and onion on medium high for 1-3 minutes, until brownish on the edges.
- Turn down the heat to medium, add tomato, and cook another 3 minutes.
- Add ground beef, stir fry on high for about 5 minutes until brown. During this time add 1/2 tablespoon of soy sauce and 1/4 teaspoon of salt.
- Reduce heat to medium and cook another 5 minutes.
- Add green beans, and stir fry on high for 5 minutes.

Putting it All Together
- After you drain your spaghetti, place them in a large bowl and add a little cooking oil (1 teaspoon or less) to keep them from sticking to each other. Not too much oil, or it will make your soup too greasy.
- Put about 4 ounces of cooked spaghetti in a serving bowl
- Add about 1 cup of beans and meat.
- Add about 1 cups of broth, or as much as you like.

Enjoy! Tibetans love to eat the bony meat from the broth on a side plate.

shaptra

Stir-Fried Meat

Every Tibetan family makes some version of *shaptra* — stir-fried meat — because it is so easy and tasty. Despite the common misconception that Tibetans are primarily vegetarian, actually they love to eat meat, though it may not be commonly eaten in the countryside in Tibet, because it is considered expensive. Traditionally, this would have been yak (*yak-sha*), beef (*lang-sha*), mutton (*lug-sha*), and goat (*ra-sha*). Nomads would be more likely to have yak, while farmers in central Tibet would eat more beef, mutton and goat, mostly because they had more access to these animals. Today, *shaptra* is most commonly made from yak, beef, mutton, or pork.

shaptra

For 2-3 people

Useful materials to have: mortar and pestle, for grinding *emma*

Ingredients
- 2 cloves garlic
- 1 tablespoon ginger
- 1 medium onion
- 1/2 medium tomato
- 3 stalks green onion
- 1 and 1/2 pounds stew beef, or any fairly lean beef of your choosing.(or mutton if your prefer)
- 1/4 teaspoon salt, or to your taste
- 1/2 tablespoon soy sauce
- 1 tablespoon cooking oil

Optional
- 1/4 teaspoon *emma* (Commonly called Szechuan pepper.)
- 1 dry red pepper

shaptra

Preparation
- Mince the garlic and ginger.
- Chop the onion, tomato and green onion.
- Cut the beef into largish bite-size chunks.
- Roughly grind the *emma* and the dried red pepper with a mortar and pestle (about 5 minutes)

Cooking
- Heat cooking oil on high in a pan suitable for stir frying.
- Turn heat down to medium high, and stir fry the onion, garlic and ginger until a little brown, 1-2 minutes.
- Add tomato and stir fry for a minute or two.
- Add meat, and stir to mix well with garlic, ginger and onions.
- Add *emma*, red pepper, soy sauce and salt, and stir to mix well.
- Stir fry everything on high for 2-3 minutes, just long enough to brown all the meat.
- Turn down the heat to medium, cover with a lid, and cook for 10-15 more minutes, stirring from time to time, until the meat is brown all the way through. (If the meat is in thinner pieces, it could take less time.)
- Just before serving, add the chopped green onion and stir briefly.
- Serve piping hot with rice, *tingmo* or *logo momo*.
- Tibetans tend to like their meat very well done, so if you like meat less well cooked, cook for less than 15 minutes.

sha mothuk

Beef Dumpling Soup

Sha mothuk is a delicious soup version of the beloved *sha momo* — meat dumpling. Tibetans love soup dishes, most likely due to a natural proclivity for warming foods at high altitude. The preparation for *sha mothuk* is fairly intensive, requiring us to not only make sha *momo*, but also the soup. Tibetans make a party out of it, gathering friends to help with the work. No matter how you make it, the taste is truly superb. And there is no better to warm you up in cold weather!

sha mothuk

For 4 people

Dough Ingredients
- 2 and 1/2 cups all-purpose flour
- ~ 1 cup cold water (from the tap)

Meat Filling Ingredients
- 1/2 stalk of celery, diced
- 1 cup cabbage, diced
- 1 tablespoon cilantro, diced
- 2 cloves garlic, minced
- 1/4 medium onion, minced (We use red onion.)
- 1 pound ground beef (We use lean ground beef, but not the most lean, because it doesn't have enough fat, and the mothuks may not be juicy enough.)
- 1/2 tablespoon salt, or to your taste
- A touch of black pepper
- 1/3 cup hot water (Need not be boiling — hot from the tap is fine)

Optional
- 1/3 cup chives, diced

sha mothuk

Broth Ingredients

- 1-2 large pieces beef bone (we used neckbone, but any bony beef is okay)
- 2 stalks celery
- 2 stalks green onions, diced
- 1/2 large tomato (1/4 is for the broth and 1/4 is for a garnish)
- 1/4 cup cilantro
- 2 cloves garlic
- 1/4 medium onion
- 1 tablespoon salt, or to your taste
- 7.5 cups water
- cooking oil

Prepare the Dough

- A little at a time, mix in about a cup of water into 2.5 cups of all-purpose flour, and knead to form a smooth ball of dough.
- Let rest, covered by a lid or in plastic for about 30 minutes.

sha mothuk

Prepare the Filling

- Everything will go into a large mixing bowl.
- Wash the celery, chives, cabbage and cilantro.
- Mince the onion and garlic.
- Dice the celery, cabbage, chives, and cilantro
- Mix 1 pound of beef, with the onion, garlic, celery, cabbage, cilantro and chives. (We do this by hand.)
- Add a touch of black pepper.
- Add 1/3 cup of hot water
- Add 1/2 tablespoon of salt
- Mix well and set aside.

Lobsang and Tsering la making mothuks in our studio kitchen :-)

sha mothuk

Prepare for the Broth
- Wash all the broth ingredients.
- Roughly chop 2 stalks of celery.
- Chop two stalks of green onion.
- Chop 1/4 cup of cilantro.
- Slice 1/4 of a large tomato.
- Dice 1/4 of a large tomato (for garnish).
- Mince 2 cloves of garlic.
- Dice 1/4 medium onion.

sha mothuk

Start Cooking the Broth
- Heat 1 tablespoon of cooking oil on high.
- Add in each item below, in the order listed, stir frying a bit (up to about 30 seconds) between each one. The temperature stays on high all the while.
    - Garlic
    - Onion
    - Celery
    - Sliced tomato
    - Beef neck bones
- Cover and let cook on high about 3 minutes.
- Add 7.5 cups of water from the tap.
- Cover and bring to a boil.
- Then turn down to a simmer while shaping the mothuks.

sha mothuk

Shape the Mothuks

- While the broth is simmering, take out the dough that has been resting and roll it out between your hands and/or on a flat surface into a long rope.
- Pinch off little roundish handfuls of dough.
- Sprinkle a little flour around your flat surface so the pieces won't stick, then press each one down with the palm of your hand. This makes circles that are thinner on the edges and thicker in the middle.
- Use a rolling pin to roll out the edges of the dough circles for the mothuks. The edges should be thinner than the center of the circle, so that when you fold the edges to make the mothuks the folded parts won't be too thick.
- Place about a tablespoon of filling in the middle of each circle.
- On the edge of the circle, push in the edge with a finger, then pinch the dough together, continuing along the outer edge of the circle. (See the video for this.)
- Note: A good example of how to shape these mothuks can be found on the *shamey* (veggie) m*othuk* video recipe.
- It is important to firmly press closed each *mothuk*. If there are openings, the fillings spill out while cooking.
- Place the mothuks on wax paper or a lightly oiled or floured surface.
- Continue making mothuks until you run out of dough or filling :-)

 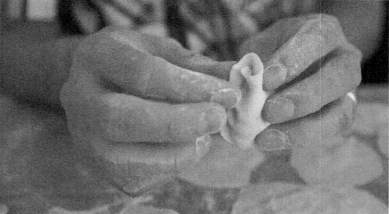

sha mothuk

Cook the Mothuks in the Soup
- Bring the simmering broth to a boil.
- Remove the neck bones from the soup, or they will break the delicate dough of the
- mothuks.
- Add 1 tablespoon of salt.
- Gently add the mothuks one at a time to the broth.
- Let the water come to a boil, and cook, covered, for 5-6 minutes, until the mothuks float to the top. Do not overcook, as this will make the meat hard.
- Stir with a wooden spoon. (Or whatever utensil you have that is less likely to tear the dough of the mothuks.)
- Turn off fire.
- Gently stir in green onion, cilantro, and diced tomato.
- Serve and enjoy!

Note:
- If you have too much meat filling, you can save it and add it to a veggie stir fry for flavor, or make a *gyathuk* with it. (Chinese-style noodle soup.)
- It's easier to use a smaller rolling pin for preparing the *mothuks* than a large one.
- Some Tibetans use only ground beef and onion and garlic for the filling, but we think this makes the filling too hard when cooked.

rutang

Basic Soup

Rutang is a very common and well-loved soup made from a variety of bony meats, which we eat with momo's, or *sha balep*, or as part of *thukpa gyathuk*. If you have time, you can let this simmer all day for maximum flavor. In Tibet, where it was normally too cold for cold drinks with one's meals, you would drink *rutang*. In the Lhasa area, the bone used for the broth would most likely be yak, or beef in the countryside.

For 2 people

Ingredients

- 1 and 1/4 pounds bony meat (We use beef chuck ribs or oxtail)
- 1 tablespoon soy sauce
- 1/2 cube beef bouillon = ~ 1 teaspoon
- 2 stalks green onion and/or 1/4 cup chopped cilantro
- 5 cups water

Optional

- 1/4 teaspoon *emma* (commonly called Szechuan pepper.)

Prepare the Soup

- Place all the broth ingredients except the green onion and cilantro in a deepish pot, on high heat. You don't need any cooking oil.

rutang

- When the soup starts to boil, turn down the heat to low, and simmer for 2-3 hours. Or, if you don't have that much time, let simmer for 30 to 40 minutes at least. Tibetans say that it should simmer all day, and the longer the better.
- Just before serving, chop your green onions and/or cilantro. Add to soup when you serve.
- Serve very hot.

That's really all there is to it. Tibetans *really* love this simple soup. :-)

shaptse

Beef with Cabbage

by Tsering Tamding la

The word "*shaptse*" means literally "meat and vegetables." In Tibet, this traditionally would have meant yak, beef or mutton meat, plus cabbage (*pedzey*), as cabbage was one of the few vegetables to grow in Tibet's high altitude. Today, of course, greenhouses and importing have brought a much greater variety of vegetables to the Tibetan diet inside Tibet. Tibetans outside of Tibet, most commonly use beef or mutton for this dish, and still frequently use cabbage, along with other vegetables. Traditionally, Tibetans would not include Tsering la's step of cooking the beef in the oven, but we like this new twist on the traditional dish.

shaptse

For 4 people

Ingredients

- 2 pounds beef (We used sirloin steak; any kind of beef, or mutton, okay.)
- 1/2 of one head of Napa cabbage (or any kind of cabbage)
- 1/2 medium onion (We used red onion.)
- 1 medium tomato
- 1/2 tablespoon salt, or to your taste
- 3 cloves garlic
- 2 stalks green onion (Called "spring onion" in video.)
- 1 tablespoon soy sauce
- 1 tablespoon cooking oil (We used Canola oil.)

shaptse

Pre-cook the Beef

- Preheat oven to 375º Fahrenheit
- Heat 1 tablespoon cooking oil on high in a skillet. (Best if you have a skillet that can be used both on the stovetop and in the oven.)
- Cook each side of the beef for two minutes on high heat.
- Transfer the skillet with the beef to the oven and cook at 375º Fahrenheit for 10 minutes. Of course if your skillet cannot go in the oven, transfer the beef to an oven-safe dish. No need to turn the beef over while cooking.

Prepare to Cook

- Wash and chop the cabbage, discarding the bottom inch or so of the stems. The stems and greens cook at different rates so keep them separate after chopping.
- Mince the garlic.
- Cut the half onion in slices.
- Chop the tomato and green onion in smallish pieces for garnish.
- Remove the beef from the oven and slice into thin slices. Save the juices from the meat in a small bowl. The beef will be pinkish at this point, but will be completely cooked through when we stir fry it with the cabbage later.

shaptse

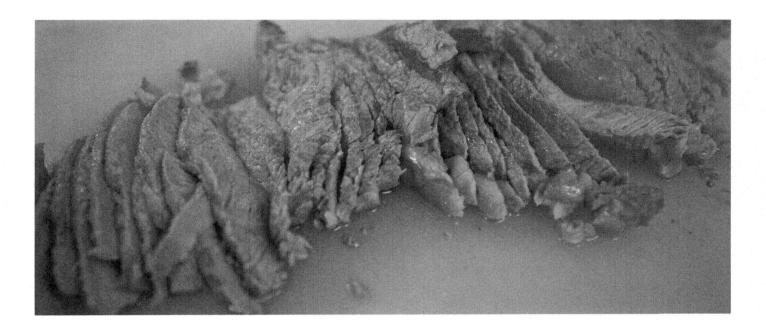

Cooking

- Heat cooking oil in skillet on high, and cook all the ingredients below on high.
- Stir fry garlic and onion for 1-3 minutes, until a little brownish on the edges.
- Add cabbage stems (the whiter part) and toss in the pan, then cook, covered, for 2-3 minutes.
- Add soy sauce and salt
- Add beef, stir, cover with lid and cook 2 minutes.
- Stir in green onions.
- Stir in leftover beef juices.
- Stir in the greens of the cabbage and tomatoes for 30 seconds or so, then take off the fire.

Serve with rice or *tingmo*.

shamdrey

Meat and Rice (and Potatoes)

In Central Tibet, *shamdrey*, meaning "meat and rice," is a popular food, especially for special celebrations, like Tibetan New Year. It is eaten basically the same inside Tibet and in the Tibetan communities outside Tibet, with both rice and potatoes. This version is beef, though yak and mutton are also commonly used. In fact, inside Tibet, it is normally cooked with mutton rib meat, with the bones included. Many people add crystal noodles – *ping* – to their *shamdrey*.

shamdrey

For 4 people

Ingredients

- 2 large potatoes
- 1/2 pound beef or mutton (we used sirloin steak.)
- 2 large bony pieces of beef or mutton (We used beef chuck ribs.)
- 2 cups rice (We used jasmine, but basmati is also common, or any kind you like.)
- 1 tablespoon minced ginger
- 3 cloves garlic, diced
- 1 medium onion, chopped
- 1/2 teaspoon cumin (*gasey*), powdered dry form
- 1 cube beef bouillon
- 1 tablespoon soy sauce
- 1 stalk green onion
- 1/2 cup cilantro, chopped
- 1 tablespoon cooking oil (We use Canola.)

Optional

- 1/4 teaspoon *emma*, ground (commonly called Szechuan pepper or prickly ash.)
- 1 oz dried water mushroom (We used "cloud ear.")

shamdrey

Prepare the Broth

- First, soak the water mushrooms in hot water for 20 minutes. (If you have time, you can soak them overnight, instead, in cold water from the tap.)
- In a pot, put 3 cups of water and the bony pieces of beef and bring to a boil, then turn down to a low boil and cook for about an hour. (This was on 2 out of 10 on our stove's setting.) Basically, the longer it cooks the better it will taste.
- One of our recipe testers, Nilanjana, found it a time saver to cook the bony beef in a pressure cooker, and then to use some but not all of the concentrated broth.
- After 1 hour, the broth had cooked a little low, so we added another cup of water, and brought the broth to a boil again before turning down to a low boil again. (If you find you like more broth in your *shamdrey*, add another 1/2 cup of water or so.)
- After soaking the mushrooms, cut or tear off the hard center or "bottom" pieces and keep the soft edges.
- Then, rinse the mushrooms very well, to get rid of stones and dirt. You will have probably half of the amount you started with, torn into bite-size pieces.
- You can add the mushrooms to the broth whenever they are ready, either at the start, along with the water and bones, or 20-30 minutes later, when you are done soaking and cleaning them. Basically, the water mushrooms can cook a very long time and still be fine, or you can add a little later, no problem.

shamdrey

Prepare Other Ingredients

- Cut the 1/2 pound of beef (we used sirloin steak) into largish, bite-sized pieces.
- Chop 1 medium onion.
- Dice 3 cloves of garlic.
- Mince 1 tablespoon of ginger.
- Grind 1/4 teaspoon of *emma* in a mortar and pestle.
- Cut the potatoes into large bite-size chunks. From one very large potato, we got about 20 pieces.
- Chop 1 stalk of green onion.
- Chop 1/2 cup of cilantro.

shamdrey

Cook the Beef

- Heat 1 tablespoon of cooking oil to high in a large pot or wok.
- Add 1/2 teaspoon of cumin and stir for a few seconds
- Add ginger, garlic, and onion and stir-fry for about 2 minutes
- Add the 1/2 pound of beef pieces, 1/4 teaspoon of ground *emma*, 1 tablespoon of soy sauce and one cube of beef bouillon.
- Cook on medium high or medium until the meat is cooked through, about 10 minutes. (Beef should be brown all the way through.)
- Now, add the bony meat broth from the other pot to your large pot or wok.
- Stir well and bring to a boil, then turn down to low (2 out of 10) and cook at a low boil for 15 minutes. (Low boil here means more than a simmer but not a rolling boil.)

Prepare the Rice

- Prepare 2 cups of uncooked rice any way that you like to cook rice. Here's what we do.
- In a rice cooker, we use 2 cups of uncooked jasmine or basmati rice (we used jasmine this time) with 1.5 cups of water from the tap. We prefer a little drier rice than usual, so you might like more water.

shamdrey

Cook the Potatoes

- Hint: Everything in this recipe can cook for a long time, except the pototoes. If they are overcooked, they will disintegrate into the broth and make it too thick. So don't add your potatoes until this stage of the cooking.
- Add the potato pieces to the broth and gently mix them well into the broth so that they will get the flavor.
- Cook for 13 minutes, or until the potatoes are tender but also not falling apart.
- Turn off fire.
- Gently stir in the green onion and cilantro. No need to cook these.

Serve

- Put as much rice as you want to eat in a soup bowl, and ladle on the *shamdrey*, giving each person a fair amount of the delicious juice.
- Some Tibetans prefer to eat their *shamdrey* and rice in separate dishes. It's up to you.
- Enjoy!

Notes

- Traditionally, the meat would be yak meat.
- The *emma* has a numbing quality on your tongue if you use too much, which some people may like but which we don't care for. If you use a tiny amount like we do here, and grind it, you get the excellent, unusual flavor without the numbing.

drothuk

Porridge with Beef

In this recipe, which comes from a family living in the countryside outside Lhasa, *"dro"* means wheat and *"thuk"* refers to *thukpa*, the general term for noodle soups and porridges. Traditionally in Tibet, *drothuk* would be made from crushed buckwheat, but since it is a challenge to find this outside of Tibet, we use oatmeal instead like many Tibetans in exile do. We use steel-cut oats instead of rolled oats because we think they are closer to the Tibetan porridge.

Drothuk can be prepared anytime in Tibet, but it is most commonly eaten as the first dish on the morning of the first day of Tibetan New Year -- *Losar*. One reason for this is that buckwheat is one of the staples of Tibetan food so eating a steaming, delicious bowl of it on *Losar* is an auspicious start for a plentiful year!

drothuk

For 2 people

Ingredients

- 1 cup steel cut oats (as a substitute for rolled buckwheat)
- 1/2 pound of beef, cut into very small pieces (We used sirloin steak. You can also use ground beef.)
- ~ 2.5 cups water
- 2 stalks green onion
- 1/2 teaspoon salt, or to your taste

drothuk

Preparation

- Chop the beef into very small pieces.
- Put 2 and 1/2 cups of water, 1/2 pound chopped beef and 1 cup of uncooked steel-cut oats in a pot.
- Turn the heat on high. Starting at this point, you will cook the porridge for about 40 minutes.
- Put the lid on and bring to a boil.
- When the water comes to a boil, turn it down very low and let it simmer for the remainder of the 40
- minutes, stirring from time to time. (After 30 minutes, the meat will probably be cooked, but the oats may need more time.)
- If the porridge is cooking at more than a simmer, turn it down to the very lowest heat, and stir more frequently.
- When done, the oats will be a bit chewy but not hard. If you like them softer, just cook a bit longer.

For Veggie Lovers

shamey momo

Steamed Vegetable Dumplings

One of the wonderful things about momos is that we can cook them so many ways. Traditionally in Central Tibet, there were only *sha* (meat) momos, but at some point in the Tibetan diaspora, vegetable fillings began to appear as well. And now, there is a wide, delicious, variety of veggie momos, including one we like at Cafe Tibet in Berkeley, California with a marscapone filling. Typical Tibetan veggie momos are stuffed with a potato filling, but Lobsang's own blend of tofu, bok choy and shiitake mushrooms, are light and delicious.

shamey momo

For 2 people (Makes about 25 momos)

Dough Ingredients

- 2 cups white all-purpose flour
- 3/4 cup water
- If you don't have time to make the dumpling wrappers yourself, you can buy round dumpling wrappers in many major grocery stores. They might also be called wonton, potsticker, gyoza or shu mai wrappers. These will taste a bit different than the kind we make, but they will work. If needed, you can also buy square wrappers and cut the corners to make them round, or just experiment with square shapes.

Filling Ingredients

- 1/2 large onion (We use red onion.)
- 1 and 1/2 tablespoons fresh ginger (Measured after mincing.)
- 4 cloves of garlic
- 1/2 cup cilantro (Measured after mincing.)
- 1 cup baby bok choy (about 2 clusters) or cabbage
- 5 ounces super firm tofu
- 2 stalks green onion
- 6 largish shiitake mushrooms (You can substitute white mushrooms.)
- 1 teaspoon salt, or to your taste
- 1 tablespoon of soy sauce
- 1/2 tablespoon vegetable bouillon
- 1/4 cup of cooking oil (We use Canola.)

shamey momo

Prepare the Dough
- Mix the white all-purpose flour and the water very well by hand and knead until you make a smooth ball of dough.
- Knead the dough very well until the dough is quite flexible. (About 5 minutes)
- Leave your dough in the pot with the lid on, or in a plastic bag, while you prepare the rest of the ingredients. You should not let the dough dry out, or it will be hard to work with.

Prepare the Filling
- Chop the onion, ginger, garlic, cilantro, bok choy, tofu, green onions and mushrooms into very, very small pieces.
- Now, you will pre-cook the tofu and mushrooms only, with the goal of cooking the water out of them.
- Heat 1/4 cup of cooking oil in a pan to high.
- Add chopped tofu, and cook on medium high for 2 minutes, until the edges are brown.
- Add chopped mushroom and cook another 3-4 minutes on medium high.
- After mushrooms and tofu have cooled, mix them very well with all the other filling ingredients.
- Cool down the mushrooms and tofu completely. If not cooled down, the green of the other vegetables will not come out correctly.

The chopped ingredients   Pre-cooking mushrooms and tofu   The mixed filling

shamey momo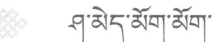

Making the *Momo* Dough Circles

When your dough and filling are both ready, it is time for the tricky part of making the dumpling shapes.

- Place the dough on a chopping board and use a rolling pin to roll it out quite thinly, about 1/8 inch thick. It should not be so thin that you can see through it when you pick it up.
- After you have rolled out the dough, you will need to cut it into little circles for each momo:
- **Method 1**: The easiest way to do this is turn a small cup or glass upside down to cut out circles about the size of the palm of your hand. We use a cup 3 and 1/3 inches in diameter. That way, you don't have to worry about making good circles of dough because each one will be the same size and shape. If you make the circles this way, you may want to thin the edges of the circle a little bit before adding the filling by pinching your way around the edge of the circle. The idea is to make the edges thinner so that when you fold the dough, there won't be a giant glob of dough on the folded places.
- **Method 2**: Of course, you can also make the circles by the more difficult traditional way. For this, first pinch off a small ball of dough. Next, use your palm to flatten out the ball. Then, flatten out the dough into a circle with a rolling pin, making the edges more thin than the middle. This method is much harder to do, and takes more time, though many Tibetans still use this method. In this case, the edges are pre-thinned so there is no need to thin them any more.
- Now that you have a small, flat, circular piece of dough, you are ready to add the filling and make the *momo* shapes. There are many different choices for *momo* shapes, but for these veggie momos we will use a very common and pretty half-moon shape. This is one of the easier shapes to make. If you want to learn about the round shape, see our *sha* (meat) *momo* recipe.

shamey momo   ཤ་མེད་མོག་མོག་

Shaping a Half-Moon *Momo*
(To do this, you will really need the video for *shamey momo*.)
- For this style, you begin by holding the flat circular dough in your left hand and putting about a tablespoon of your veggie filling in the middle of the dough. It can be challenging if you put too much, so at first you may want to start with a little less filling.
- Beginning anywhere on the circle, pinch the edge of the dough together. Now you will fold in a small piece of dough from the "top" edge of the circle and pinching it down against the "bottom" edge of the circle. (Where the "bottom" half of the circle is the half facing you when the *momo* is in your hands.) The "bottom" edge of the circle — the edge nearest you — stays relatively flat, and doesn't get folded. All the folding happens only on one side of the *momo*. Continue folding and pinching from the starting point, moving along the edge until you reach the other tip of the half-moon. The important point is to close all the openings well so that you don't lose the juice while cooking.
- As you are making your momos, you will need to have a non-stick surface and a damp cloth or lid handy to keep the momos you've made from drying out while you're finishing the others. You can lay the momos in the lightly-greased trays of your steamer and keep the lid on them, or you can lay them on wax paper and cover them with the damp cloth.
- Note: If you prefer, you can make the round *momo* shape we used for sha *momo*.

shamey momo

shamey momo

Cook up Your Momos!

- Finally, you should boil water in a large steamer. (Tibetans often use a double-decker steamer, to make many momos at one time.)
- Oil the steamer surface lightly before putting the momos in, so they won't stick to the metal. We use spray oil.
- Place the momos a little distance apart in the steamer as they will expand a little bit when they cook. They should not be touching.
- Add the momos after the water is already boiling.
- Steam the momos for 10-12 minutes, with the water boiling on high heat.
- As long as the dough is cooked, they are done, as the veggie filling really hardly needs to cook more.

Serving

- Serve the momos right off the stove, with the dipping sauce of your choice. At home, we mix together soy sauce and Patak's Lime Relish, which we get in Indian stores, or the Asian section of supermarkets. Tibetan hot sauce is also very good – see our *sepen* recipe.
- Be careful when you take the first bite of the hot momos since the juice is very, very hot, and can burn you easily.

shamey balep

Fried Vegetable Pies

The name *shamey balep* – "non-meat bread" – doesn't sound anywhere near as mouth-wateringly delicious as the real thing. Hot and juicy, our veggie *balep* are filled with tofu, mushrooms and bok choy, and are much more healthy than their better-known meat cousins, the *sha balep*. Veggie *balep*, like veggie momos, are a relatively new development for Tibetans, who traditionally are heavy meat eaters. The increasing health and humanitarian awareness of Tibetans in the diaspora has lead to the slow growth of Tibetan vegetarianism, especially among young Tibetans.

shamey balep

For 2 people (about 10 balep each, plenty for leftovers :-)

Dough Ingredients
- 2 and 1/2 cups all purpose flour
- A little less than one cup of cold water (Tap water is fine.)
- Pre-made dumpling wrappers would not work very will for *shamey balep*

Filling Ingredients
- 10 ounces very firm plain tofu diced very small
- 1 ounce dried shiitake mushrooms, soaked and chopped very small (White mushrooms okay.)
- 2 cups chopped baby bok choy. (Or Napa cabbage, or other cabbage or greens)
- 1/4 cup minced ginger
- 2 level tablespoons of minced garlic
- 1/2 cup chopped cilantro
- 1 stalk green onion
- 1 cup chopped onion (we like red onion)
- 1 tablespoon of soy sauce
- 1/2 teaspoon of salt, or to your taste
- 1 tablespoon of veggie bouillon
- 1.5 tablespoons of oil for pre-cooking the tofu for the filling
- 2 tablespons of cooking oil (we use canola oil) to fry the balep.
- 1/4 cup of cooking oil to stir-fry the tofu and mushrooms

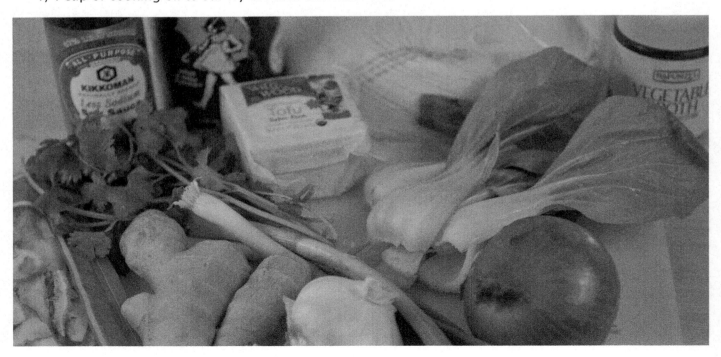

shamey balep

Soak the Mushrooms
- Boil enough water to cover your mushrooms and soak for 30 minutes.

Prepare the Dough
- Measure out the dough into a largish bowl, then stir in a little less than a cup of water. Dribble in the water slowly while mixing with your hand, to form a smooth ball.
- Place dough in a dish with a lid, or cover with plastic, or put in a plastic bag.
- Let the dough rest while you are preparing the *balep* filling. We rest the dough so that it will be softer when shaping the *balep*.
- Ultimately you want the dough to be soft enough to roll out and to stick together when you pinch together the edges of the *balep*, and hard enough to form a smooth ball and not to stick to the rolling surface. Don't worry too much if your dough is too hard or too soft. If too soft you can add some more flour and/or put more flour on your rolling surface. If it's too hard, you can add more water and re-knead. You don't have to let it rest any longer in that case.

shamey balep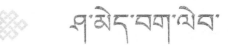

Prepare the Tofu and Mushrooms
- Drain, if needed, the tofu and chop very small.
- After your mushrooms have soaked, drain them well, squeezing out as much excess water as you can, and chop very small.
- Heat 1/4 cup of cooking oil in a pan to high.
- Stir fry the tofu and mushrooms together on high heat for 5 minutes. The tofu should be a bit brown. The goal here is to cook excess moisture out so that your *balep* won't be soggy.
- Set aside the cooked tofu and mushroom mixture until it cools to room temperature.

Roll out the Dough
- Roll out the dough on a lightly floured surface with a rolling pin to about 1/8 inch thickness.
- Use an inverted glass or cup to cut out circles that are about 3 and 1/2 inches in diameter. Set the circles of dough aside. You might want to put them on waxed paper or a lightly floured surface.
- As you cut out the circles you will be left with the dough outside the circles. Pick it back up, form it into a ball and repeat rolling it out until you have nothing left.
- Note: Many Tibetans make the circles one by one by making a small ball of dough and then rolling out each one, but we're lazy and we're not good at rolling them out one by one, so we use the cup method.

shamey balep

Fill and Shape the *Balep*

- Place a heaping tablespoon or so of filling on one circle of dough, then place a second circle of dough on top of the first one.
- Pinch the edges together very firmly— going all around the circle.
- Then, start anywhere on the circle, fold over a small piece of the edge, and pinch it down, repeating this all around the circle.

Keep the *balep* you have finished on a lightly oiled flat dish or surface, to avoid the dough sticking on the surface. If the *balep* are going to be sitting for a long time, you can place a damp cloth over them to keep them from drying out.

shamey balep

Cook
- Heat 2 tablespoons of oil in a large pan until oil is very hot and then place one layer of *balep* in the pan and and lower heat to medium. You don't want to burn the outsides before the inside is cooked.
- Cook until golden brown on both sides, turning frequently, about 4-5 minutes per side total.
- Be prepared to turn the fan on or to open the windows as the cooking process can be quite greasy and hot.

Serve
- *Balep* go well with something light, like *trang tsel*.
- They are delicious with Patak's lime relish [http://www.pataks.co.uk/products/] or Tibetan hot sauce mixed with some soy sauce.

shamey tsel

"Meatless" Vegetables (Mushrooms and Cabbage)

It tells you something about Tibetan cuisine that a basic veggie dish like *shamey tsel* translates as "meatless vegetables." Literally, it is *sha* (meat) + *mey* (without) + *tsel* (vegetables). Because few vegetables grow in the high-altitude farmlands of Tibet without the help of greenhouses, Tibetans traditionally ate few vegetables. The vegetables that are grown and eaten tend to be hardy: cabbage, radish, turnip, carrot, potato, onion, radish, and celery. *Shamey tsel* could be any of these veggies, but Lobsang's tasty version is a cabbage dish beautifully flavored by shiitake mushrooms.

shamey tsel

For 2 people

Ingredients

- 10 ounces Napa cabbage
- 6 large shiitake mushrooms. (You can substitute white mushrooms.)
- 2 cloves garlic
- 1/2 large onion
- 1 large tomato
- 1/4 teaspoon salt, or to your taste
- 1/2 tablespoon soy sauce
- 1 tablespoon cooking oil (We used Canola.)

shamey tsel

Preparation

- Clean mushrooms with a damp cloth or paper towel.
- Roughly chop the mushrooms, discarding the stems.
- Chop and wash the cabbage (Separate the stems and greens after you chop them, because they cook at different rates)
- Mince the garlic.
- Roughly chop the tomato and onion.

shamey tsel

Cooking

- Heat cooking oil in a skillet on high.
- Stir fry garlic and onion on medium high until the edges are lightly browned.
- Add tomato, salt and soy sauce and cook for 2-3 minutes on medium high.
- Add mushrooms, mix well and cook for 5 minutes on medium low.
- Add cabbage stems, and stir fry for about 2 minutes.
- Add the cabbage greens and stir fry another minute.
- Serve with rice or *tingmo*.

shamey mothuk

Vegetable Dumplings in Soup

By Tsering Tamding la

Shamey mothuk is another in a fine line of superb variations on the *momo* (dumpling) theme. Here, we fill the momos with tofu, shiitake mushrooms, bok choy and spinach, and then cook them in a savory broth, for a doubly wonderful flavor. When momos are served in soup, they are called *mothuk*. You'll need time to make these, and we recommend inviting some friends over to fold the momos and cook together. When we are making momos, we turn up the Tibetan music, chat and have a lot of fun. And they taste great!

shamey mothuk

For 3 people (about 15 mothuks plus soup)

Dough Ingredients
- 1 and 1/4 cups all-purpose flour
- 1/2 cup cold water (from the tap)

Veggie/Vegan Filling Ingredients
- 3 large shiitake mushrooms. (You can substitute white mushrooms.) = ~ 1 ½ cups diced
- 1 stalk celery, diced
- 1/4 large tomato, diced = 2 tablespoons
- 1 stalk green onion
- 2 cloves garlic, minced
- 5 ounces very firm tofu, diced
- 1/4 medium onion, minced (We use red.)
- ~ 1 cup baby bok choy (2 smallish pieces), diced
- 1 cup spinach, diced (As long as they are clean, no need to remove stems.)
- 1 teaspoon salt, or to your taste
- 1 tablespoon soy sauce
- 1 tablespoon cooking oil for pan frying (We use Canola.)

shamey mothuk

Ingredients for Broth
- 1 clove garlic, sliced
- 1/4 medium onion, sliced
- 1 stalk celery, diced
- 3 large shiitake mushrooms, cut in half and then sliced (You can substitute white mushrooms.)
- 1/4 large tomato, diced for garnish
- 1 and 1/2 tablespoon cilantro, chopped
- 2 cups spinach, roughly chopped (keep the stems and greens separate as they cook at different rates.)
- 2 tablespoons chives, diced
- 6 cups water
- 1 tablespoon soy sauce
- 1 tablespoon salt, or to your taste
- 1 tablespoon cooking oil

Prepare the Dough
- Combine the dough and water, kneading until you have a fairly smooth ball of dough.
- The dough may be a bit on the dry side.
- Let rest, covered by a lid or in plastic for about 30 minutes.

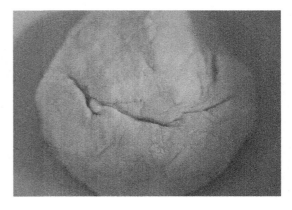

shamey mothuk

Prepare the Filling
- First, dice or mince all the filling ingredients
- Heat 1 tablespoon of oil in a pan to high.
- Stir fry on high heat all the filling ingredients, in this order:
  - Garlic and onion, about 1 minute.
  - Add celery, 1-2 minutes.
  - Tofu, about 3 more minutes.
  - Mushrooms, soy sauce, 1-2 minutes.
  - Baby bok choy, 1 minute.
  - Spinach, 1 minute.
  - Then quickly stir in salt, tomato, and green onion, 30 seconds to 1 minute.
  - Turn off fire and let cool to room temperature.

The filling ingredients, chopped.

The filling while cooking.

Start the Broth
- On high, heat 1 tablespoon of cooking oil.
- Stir fry onion and garlic until a little brown, about a minute.
- Add celery and mushrooms, and stir fry 1-2 more minutes.
- Add 6 cups of water.
- Add 1 tablespoon of salt and 1 tablespoon of soy sauce.
- Cover soup with lid, bring to a boil.
- Turn down to a simmer while preparing the mothuks.

shamey mothuk

Shape the Mothuks

- While the broth is simmering, take out the dough that has been resting and roll it out between your hands into the shape of a long rope.
- Pinch off pieces of dough.
- Sprinkle a little flour around so the pieces won't stick, then press each one down with the palm of your hand. This makes thinner on the edges and thicker in the middle.
- Use a rolling pin to make the edges of the mothuks thin. The edges should be thinner than the center of the circle, so that when you fold the edges to make the mothuks, the folded parts won't be too thick.
- Place about a tablespoon of filling in the middle of each circle.
- On the edge of the circle, push in the edge with a finger, then pinch the dough together, continuing along the outer edge of the circle. (See the video for this.)
- Place the mothuks on wax paper or a lightly oiled or floured surface.
- Continue making mothuks until you run out of dough or filling :-)

shamey mothuk

Make the Soup

- Important: Bring the simmering broth to a boil. Don't add the dumplings before your broth is boiling or they will likely break while cooking.
- Gently add the mothuks one at a time.
- Let the water come to a boil again after they have been added, then cook about 4 minutes on high.
- When mothuks float to the top, stir in the spinach stems first.
- Use a wooden spoon, or whatever utensil you have that is less likely to tear the delicate dough of the mothuks.
- Turn off the fire.
- Add spinach greens, chives, cilantro and tomato and gently stir all together.
- Serve and enjoy!

Note

- If you have too much filling, you can save it and eat it as a vegetable with rice or add some to the soup at the end to make the broth even more delicious.
- It's easier to use a smaller rolling pin for preparing the mothuks than a large one.

Basic Fresh Salad

By Tsering Tamding la

Trang tsel literally means "cold vegetables" and is the Tibetan version of a fresh salad. Cold foods are quite rare in high, cold Tibet, where fresh vegetables have not traditionally been available, and *trang tsel* is not something that most Tibetans inside Tibet have ever commonly eaten. This is more a modern addition to Tibetan cuisine, and will vary according to the tastes of the maker. Tsering Tamding la has created a beautiful version with a refreshingly simple earthy and yet fresh flavor.

trang tsel

For 3-4 people

Ingredients
- 1 cucumber (We used English cucumber, but any kind would be okay except pickling cucumbers.)
- 1 medium tomato (We used Roma.)
- 1 medium onion
- 1 small beet

Ingredients for Dressing
- Juice of 1 lemon (with seeds removed)
- 1/2 tablespoon olive oil
- Salt to taste
- Black pepper to taste

Preparation

- Thinly slice the cucumber and tomato in circles.
- Slice a red onion into extra-thin circles. (You can use other onions, but red makes the salad more attractive.)
- Peel the beet and slice into thin circles.
- Cut the lemon for the dressing in half. Squeeze the lemon's juice into a small bowl.
- Add about 1/2 tablespoon of olive oil.
- Add black pepper to taste.
- Add salt to taste.
- Stir the dressing well.
- Arrange the slices of cucumber, tomato, onion and beet on a plate.
- Drizzle the dressing over the salad.

Serve as a cool, fresh accompaniment for any of the heavier meat dishes, especially momos.

A Little Something for Everyone

thenthuk

"Pull" Noodle Soup

Thenthuk" (pronounced roughly like "ten" + "too" + k) is a typical Tibetan noodle soup that keeps the nomads warm during the long Tibetan winters. You can make it either with vegetables or meat. In Tibetan "then" means pull and "*thuk*" means noodles. We hope the video will help you be able to make a great *"thenthuk"* :-) Note that the initial cooking of the broth happens quickly, so best to have all your ingredients prepared before you start actually cooking.

thenthuk

For 2 people

You can make this vegetarian-style, or with meat.

Dough Ingredients
- 1 cup all-purpose flour
- 1/2 cup of water

Broth Ingredients
- About 1 and 1/2 tablespoons cooking oil (We used olive oil.)
- 2 cloves garlic, minced
- 1 tablespoon of ginger, minced
- 1/2 medium onion (We use red.)
- 1 medium tomato, chopped
- 2 and 1/2 cups water, for soup (If you like a thinner broth, add more water.)
- 1 tablespoon of soy sauce
- 1/3 teaspoon of bouillon (Vegetable bouillon for veg version — any meat bouillon for meat version.)
- 2 cups spinach (Or as much as you like.)
- 1/2 cup chopped cilantro and/or 2 stalks of green onion, chopped

Optional
- 3/4 of 1 medium-large daikon
- 1 tablespoon of salt, for rinsing the daikon

For Meat Version, Add
- 1/2 pound of beef or mutton (We use stew beef but pretty much any kind is okay.)
- Optional: 1/2 teaspoon ground *emma* (Commonly called Sechuan pepper and used only for meat version, not for vegetable version.)

thenthuk

The Dough

The dough is very important for this noodle soup. It needs to sit for 15 or 20 minutes so that it can become flexible and easy to pull.

- Slowly add about 1/2 cup of water to 1 cup of all-purpose flour in a bowl.
- Mix the flour and water very well by hand and keep adding water until you can make a smooth ball of dough. Then knead the dough very well until the dough is flexible, 3-5 minutes. You want it both solid and flexible enough to stretch rather than break when pulled.
- Roll the dough between your hands to make a thick rope shape, and break that long piece into 4-5 shorter pieces of the same thickness.
- Put oil on your hand and roll the pieces between your hands again so they won't stick together.
- Put the 4-5 pieces of dough in a plastic bag or in a pot and put a lid to cover the dough so it doesn't dry out.
- Let rest, covered, for 15-20 minutes.

  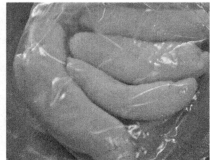

thenthuk

The Broth

Now the dough is prepared and you can start the broth.

- If using daikon, peel and chop it. Cover the chopped daikon with water and add 1 tablespoon of salt. Soak the daikon in this salty water, stirring around with your hand, then rinse well. Tibetans say this takes the strong "radish smell" away.
- Chop the onion, ginger, garlic, and tomato.
- Optional: If you are cooking the meat version, cut it into thin bite-size slices.
- Heat 1 and 1/2 tablespoons of oil on high heat until hot.
- Turn down heat to medium high and stir fry onion, ginger, and garlic for 2-3 minutes until the edges are a little brown.
- Add the beef, and raising the heat back up to high, stir fry for 3-4 minutes, or until the meat is well browned.
- When meat is brown, add tomatoes, and cook covered, still on high for 2-3 more minutes.
- Add beef or vegetable bouillon, and soy sauce.
- Optional: Add the *emma*, if you are cooking the meat version.
- At this time, you can add the daikon, and cook, still on high, another 2-3 minutes.
- Add two and a half cups of water to the pot.
- Bring the broth to a boil, stirring occasionally.
- While the soup is cooking, chop 1/2 cup of cilantro, two green onions, and 2 cups of spinach (Or as much as you like).

thenthuk

Making the "Pull" Noodles

- When the broth starts to boil, you can add the dough. Take a wedge of dough and roll it between your hands so it gets a little longer. Flatten it with your fingers. Then pull the dough off in little flat pieces as long as your thumb and throw them in the pot. See how fast you can pull off the noodles :-)
- When all the noodles are in the pot, cook it for an additional three to five minutes to cook the noodles. After that, you can put in the cilantro, green onions, and spinach. They don't need to cook, really, so you can serve the soup immediately.
- Enjoy your *thenthuk* and sweat because it really makes you warm!

pa

Tsampa Dish

Tsampa, the most uniquely Tibetan of all Tibetan foods, is a hearty, nutty-tasting flour made from roasted barley. The most common way to eat *tsampa* is to mix it by hand with butter tea, dried *dri* (the female of the yak species) cheese and sometimes sugar, to form a dough. In this form it is called, simply, *pa*, and for many Tibetans in the past, *pa* was eaten three times a day, every day. Today, it is less common to find those who eat only *pa*, but it is still a common food in Central Tibet, and for travellers, who bring a leather pouch for mixing the ingredients on the road.

pa

For 1 person

Ingredients

- 1 and 1/4 cup *tsampa* (Roasted barley flour.)
- 1/2 cup hot black tea, or butter tea (*po cha*), or just hot water. We use Lipton's, or loose black Indian tea.
- 2-3 tablespoons butter (Do not use if you use butter tea.)

Optional:

- 1/2 tablespoon sugar
- Dried cheese from the female yak — *dri* cheese.

Preparation

- Add hot black tea and butter (as well as sugar and dried cheese if you like) into a single serving bowl.
- Add the *tsampa*, and mix well by hand, turning the bowl as you mix, until you can form fist fulls of doughy pieces to eat.

Notes

- The video is a little incorrect— we added too much tea, and had to add 1 and 1/4 cups of *tsampa* instead of 1 cup as we may have said in the video.

sepen

Hot Sauce

By Nyima la and Kelsang la

You would be hard pressed to have a meal in Lhasa, and in Tibetan communities in exile, without being offered a healthy serving of fiery Tibetan hot sauce. While Tibetan food itself is very rarely spicy, Tibetans love to spice up whatever they are eating with dollops of the sauce. And that really means anything, including *balep korkun* (pan bread) or even *pa* (*tsampa* with butter tea)! The sauces vary, and some include more of a tomato base, or some kind of greens. This recipe, an extremely easy, fast and fantastic one, comes to us from our friends, *sepen* masters Nyima la and Kelsang la. Be careful, this is extremely hot!

sepen

Ingredients

- 1 cup dried whole red peppers (We don't have a special brand we're attached to – of course different peppers will each have different heat, so this part is always an experiment!)
- 1/2 cup fresh cilantro (including most of the stems)
- 2 medium cloves garlic (2 teaspoons minced garlic)
- 2 inches of fresh ginger (2 tablespoons minced ginger)
- (Optional) 1 teaspoon whole pods of *emma* or *yerma*, ground.

sepen

Preparation

- Soak the red pepper in cold water overnight, or if you don't have much time, in very hot water for 20 to 30 minutes.
- Drain the water.
- Mince the garlic and ginger.
- If you are using *emma*, grind it in a mortar and pestle for a few minutes. You don't want large pieces since a large piece will numb you, but it does not need to be ground to a powder. Just somewhere between whole and powder.
- Chop the cilantro, including most of the stems. (We cut off and discard just the tip of the stem.)
- Add all ingredients in a blender or just grind them in a mortar and pestle. (Tip: The hot sauce can leave a smell on a plastic blender or food processor. On ours, the smell "aired out" out after a few days with the lid off.) If you are using a mortar and pestle, it helps to finely chop the soaked peppers first.
- Blend until the sauce reaches the desired consistency. If it is too thick for you, just add small amounts of water until it reaches the consistency you like.
- Serve with momo's, *sha baglep*, or, if you are Tibetan, just about anything! :-)

sepen ཞེ་པན་

po cha

Tibetan (Butter) Tea

For most people, Tibetan butter tea is an acquired taste, since it is savory rather than sweet, and has a completely unexpected flavor. Many non-Tibetans don't care for it much at first, but come to love it when it is associated with warmth on a cold day and good times spent with Tibetan friends, or the adventure of travel in Tibet or Tibetan communities in India or Nepal. Some non-Tibetans find it helpful to think of it as a sort of light soup rather than as tea. This way, your mind isn't so shocked when you drink it!

po cha

How Tibetans Traditionally Make Butter Tea

In Tibet, the process of making butter tea takes a long time and is pretty complicated. People use a special black tea that comes from an area called Pemagul in Tibet. The tea comes in bricks of different shapes, and we crumble off some tea and boil it for many hours. We save the liquid from the boiling and then whenever we want to make tea, we add some of that liquid, called *chaku*, to our boiling water. For the butter and milk, Tibetans used to, and still do, use butter and milk from the female of the yak species. Though people talk about "yak" butter and milk, the correct term is actually "*dri*" butter and milk, because a yak is a male, while butter and milk come from the female, the *dri*.

Preparing the Tea

Lucky for us, it is much easier to make *po cha* nowadays. Most Tibetan people who live outside of Tibet use Lipton tea, or some kind of plain black tea. You can use any kind of milk you want, though I think the full fat milk is the best, and sometimes I use Half & Half, which is half cream and half milk.

You will need: One blender, churn or large container with a tight lid.

po cha

For 2 people

Ingredients
- 4 cups of water
- Plain black tea (2 individual teabags, like Lipton's black tea, or two heaping spoons of loose black tea)
- 1/4 teaspoon salt, or to your taste
- 2 tablespoons butter (salted or unsalted)
- 1/3 cup Half & Half or milk

Preparation
- Bring four cups of water to a boil.
- Put two bags of tea or two heaping tablespoon of loose tea in the water and let boil for two minutes minutes. (For stronger tea, add a tea bag, or another tablespoon of loose tea.)
- Add a heaping 1/4 teaspoon of salt.
- Take out the tea bags or if you use loose tea, strain the tea grounds.
- Add 1/3 cup of milk or Half & Half.
- Now turn off the stove.
- Pour your tea mixture, along with two tablespoons of butter, into a blender, or any container with a tight lid. (We use a plastic churn that we have not seen for sale anywhere, but most Tibetans use a blender.)
- Churn, blend or shake the mixture for two or three minutes. In Tibet, we think the *po cha* tastes better if you churn it longer.

Important Note
Serve the tea right away, since *po cha* is best when it's very hot!

thukpa bhathuk

"*Bhatsa*" Noodle Soup

Thukpa bhathuk centers on the little hand-rolled *bhatsa* noodles that most resemble, in their shape, Italian gnocchi, but with an extra little scoop. One of the benefits of this shape is that you get a little extra taste of the broth with every bite of *bhatsa*. Like other Tibetan noodle soups, *thukpa bhathuk* is especially popular in winter. It's relatively easy and quick, and wonderfully warming on a cold day. Tibetans traditionally use mutton, beef or yak for the meat, but it is also delicious in it's veggie incarnation, for which you just leave out the meat and use vegetable bouillon for the broth.

thukpa bhathuk

For 2 people

Soup Ingredients
- 9 ounces beef (We used sirloin steak but you can use any beef suitable for stew.)
- 2 cloves garlic, minced
- 1/3 medium onion (We used red.)
- 1 cube beef bouillon
- 3 cups water (first cooking) + 3 cups of water (second cooking)
- 2/3 of a large daikon, chopped (Japanese radish)
- 1 stalk green onion, chopped
- 1 cup cilantro, chopped
- 5 cups spinach (measure before chopping), roughly chopped. (As long as they are clean, no need to remove the stems.)
- 1 tomato, chopped

Dough Ingredients
- 1 and 1/2 cups all-purpose white flour
- ~1/2 cup water

thukpa bhathuk

First Cooking of the Soup
- Chop the beef into smallish bite-size pieces.
- Mince the garlic.
- Chop the onion.
- Boil the beef in 3 cups of water with bouillon, garlic and onion.
- When the broth starts to boil, turn down to medium and cook for 20 minutes.
- After 20 minutes, turn down to low, and cook for another 30 minutes.
- The longer you cook this soup, basically, the better, though 50 minutes is fine.

Prepare the Daikon
- Peel the daikon (a potato peeler works well) and chop off the two ends.
- Chop the daikon into thin, narrow strips about as long as your finger. The strips should be about as thin and narrow as you can make them.
- Soak the chopped daikon in water with ~ 1 teaspoon of salt
- Soak for a few minutes, swishing around with your hand.
- Rinse well, several times, to get rid of salt and bitterness.
- Tibetans say that rinsing like this gets rid of the strong radish smell.

thukpa bhathuk

Chop the Garnishes
- Chop the tomato into smallish pieces.
- Finely chop the cilantro.
- Chop the green onion.
- Roughly chop the spinach (or don't chop if you like large pieces)
- Set all these aside until the soup is almost done.

thukpa bhathuk

Prepare the Dough
- Slowly add the water to the flour.
- Mix to form a smooth ball and then knead a couple of minutes.
- This dough does not have to rest after kneading so you can prepare it any time during the cooking process.

Shape the Dough
- First, rub the ball of dough between your hands to make it into a thick tube of dough, and then pinch off pieces of that tube to make 4-5 chunks of dough.
- Then rub each piece of dough between your hands to form long, thin ropes of dough.
- Pinch off a piece as big as the end of your fingernail, or smaller.
- Rub the dough with one finger in the palm of your hand to cause the little piece of dough to curl up (the better to scoop up the juices in the soup). These little scooped pieces of dough are your *bhatsa*.
- Repeat until you've used up all your ropes of dough.
- You can sprinkle a little flour around the pile of *bhatsa*, to keep them from sticking together.

 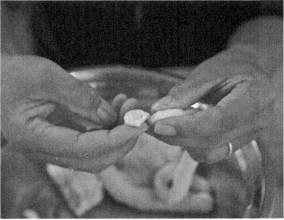 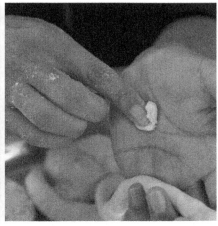

thukpa bhathuk

Final Cooking

- Add another 3 cups of water to the soup and bring to a boil.
- When soup starts to boil again, add daikon and cook for 2-3 minutes
- Now add all the little pieces of dough — the bhatsa — and cook for another 5 minutes. When cooked the *bhatsa* will pop up to the surface of the soup.
- Add spinach, cilantro, green onion, and tomato, and serve right away. (These final ingredients do not really need to cook, and look nicer if they are fresh looking.)

Notes

For a veggie version, leave out the meat and substitute vegetable bouillon.

Sweets

dresil

Sweet Rice

Dresil is a lightly sweet dish that is typically served on special occasions. In Central Tibet, people eat it in the morning on the first day of Tibetan *Losar* — New Year, and also for other special occasions, like weddings or special Buddhist holidays.

Traditionally, Tibetans eat the *dresil* with *droma*, sugar, and *dri* (female yak) butter. Droma is "a small root, which grows on grasslands throughout Tibet."(www.terma.org/shambhalasun052004.pdf). It tastes a little like sweet potato.

Our recipe includes an option to use *droma*, but don't worry if you don't have access to it — the dish will still be authentic as many Tibetans outside of Tibet commonly make their *dresil* without *droma*. We also use cow's butter rather than butter from a *dri*, and leave out the sugar, as the raisins give a nice light sweetness, though most Tibetans do use sugar. On the first *Losar* morning, we often make a really special *dresil* with a few other dried fruits and nuts, like dried cherries, pecans and pine nuts.

dresil

Ingredients

- 2 cups rice (Before cooking. We used basmati, but almost any rice is okay.)
- 6 tablespoons butter (salted or unsalted)
- 1/2 cup cashew nuts (We use unsalted.)
- 1 cup raisins
- 1/4 cup sugar (if desired)
- Any other nuts or dried fruits, as desired

Optional

- 1 cup *droma*

Preparation

- Cook the rice. For the rice, for 2 cups of basmati, you should use 3.5 cups of water, not 4 as it originally says in the video.
- If using *droma*, boil the *droma* in 3-4 cups of water for 35-40 minutes until softened but not mushy. Drain and rinse well because most *droma* will have a fair amount of soil in it.
- Mix together all the ingredients
- Serve in small bowls and enjoy with sweet tea or *po cha* — butter tea.

bhatsa marku

Bhatsa Noodles with Sweet Butter Sauce

Tibetans are famously non-vegetarian, but there are times when many Tibetans refrain from eating meat, such as during the holy month of *Saka Dawa*, commemorating Buddha's birth, enlightenment, teaching and death day. During this time, *bhatsa marku* becomes especially popular. This dish, sort of like a sweet, extremely rich macaroni and cheese, can be too buttery for Western palates, though our recipe testers have really enjoyed the mix of sweet with the cheese. You might experiment with less butter, though Tibetans themselves really love the heavy butteriness. Cooks in Central Tibet would traditionally use dried cheese from the female yak (*dri*), which does not melt down and get stringy when it is hot as much as Romano or Parmesan do. We have not been able to replicate the way that *dri* cheese coats the *bhatsa* without melting down a bit, but the good news is that it still tastes great when the cheese melts :-)

Bhatsa marku made with *chuship* — *dri* cheese.

bhatsa marku

For one person

Ingredients
- 1 cup all-purpose flour
- 1/4 cup water
- 1 to 3 tablespoons butter (Traditionally, Tibetans add a lot!)
- 1/2 cup dried *dri* cheese, or 1/3 cup Romano, Parmesan or other hard cheese
- 1 to 1 and 1/2 tablespoons sugar

bhatsa marku

Prepare the *Bhatsa*

- Mix 1 cup of all-purpose flour and 1/4 cup of water
- Mix the flour and water by hand and knead to form a smooth ball of dough.
- Shape the ball of dough with your hands into a long rope shape.
- Pinch off small pieces of dough, and then rub each piece of dough into the palm of your hand to fold it over to a curved shape. (Alternatively, you can just make a very thin rope of dough — about the size of your index finger — and then cut off very small pieces with a knife. The pieces should be as big as the end of your index fingernail. No need to rub these in your palm. You can just cook the cut pieces.)
- If the little dough pieces — the *bhatsa* — stick together, just add a tiny bit of flour to them and shake them around in the bowl to help keep them separated.

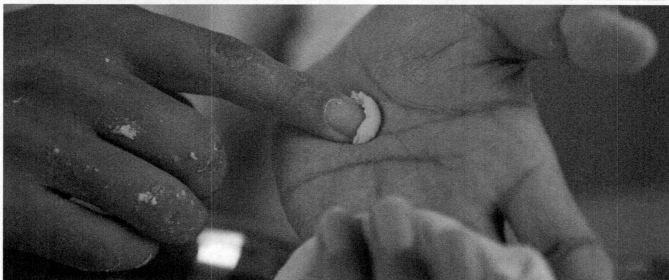

bhatsa marku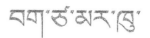

Cook

- Boil 4 cups of water.
- When the water starts to boil, add all the little *bhatsa* to the pot.
- Cook for 5-6 minutes, or until the *bhatsa* are cooked. When cooked, they rise to the top of the water, and should not be doughy on the inside. (May need to cook longer than 5-6 minutes on your stove.)
- Drain the water from the pot.
- Using the same pot, add 1 and 1/2 tablespoons of sugar, 1/2 cup *dri* cheese or 1/3 cup of Romano or other hard cheese (like Parmesan), and 3 tablespoons of butter.
- Mix well and eat hot.

Notes

- If you leave the sugar out, and cut the butter by half or more, it is a nice, unusual, homemade Mac and Cheese :-)
- For a sugar-free version: you can substitute raisins or dates for the sugar.

Acknowledgements — Thuk Je Che!

We would like to thank, first and foremost, master Tibetan Chef Tsering Tamding la, who generously contributed both recipes and a considerable amount of time to *Tibetan Home Cooking*. Tsering la came over to our home studio twice for marathon taping days and, as you will see in the videos, is not only a superb cook, but also a charming spokesperson for Tibetan cooking. Thanks, Tsering la, for the fantastic food, and the fun!

If you live in the San Francisco Bay Area, we recommend Tsering la to cater your parties. He has experience with a wide range of cuisines, besides Tibetan including Italian, Indian and Ghanian! Contact us at yowangdu@yowangdu.com for Tsering la's information.

Thanks also to our friends Nyima la and Kelsang la, for the great *sepen* (Tibetan hot sauce) recipe, page 116. Lobsang has always considered this hot sauce to be one of the best he's ever had :-)

To our wonderful, talented recipe testers — thank you! It was such a pleasure to interact with our early testers: Jennie Berthet from www.healthwithjen.com, Nilanjana Moulick, Michele, Ross Bennetts, Kathleen Wong, Kyle Riff, Karolina, Amanda Nichols, and Annapurna Ghosh, who all kindly volunteered to test the *Tibetan Home Cooking* recipes pre-launch, and who generously shared detailed feedback, and even photos of their work.

Thanks, Chantal Guillemin, for generously offering to copyedit the eBook — you're so kind!

A big thanks to our friend Tony Kaplan, documentary filmmaker, who shared with us tips on cameras and shooting.

And last but not least, we'd like to thank you! The greatest pleasure in creating a Tibetan culture website (www.yowangdu.com) and a book about Tibetan home cooking has been, without a doubt, our interactions with our readers. You keep us going and make it all fun. Thank you!

About the Authors

Lobsang Wangdu, the primary chef for these recipes, learned to cook at a young age by watching his aunt and uncle in Tibet. As he grew older, he assisted experienced Tibetan chefs, asking questions while he helped cook. Lobsang has been making variations on the recipes in this book for well over twenty years, and has become a Tibetan chef in his own right, with a wealth of experience and a passion for making the people he cooks for happy. Lobsang is also a webmaster and digital photographer, who is as much at home in front of a computer as he is a stove. He runs the www.yowangdu.com website and also served as photographer, graphic designer and camera person for *Tibetan Home Cooking*.

Yolanda O'Bannon served as writer, editor, photographer, camera person and video editor for *Tibetan Home Cooking*. She is passionate about Tibet, Tibet travel and preserving Tibetan culture. Traveling extensively ever since her childhood as an Air Force brat, she has lived in France, Libya, Spain, Japan and India. She is also a web producer and SEO strategist, and runs YoWangdu Experience Tibet (www.yowangdu.com) with Lobsang.

Lobsang and Yolanda are married and live in the San Francisco Bay Area, where they love to cook and eat Tibetan food :-)

Made in the USA
Monee, IL
12 June 2021